SURVIVING IN BMORE

A REAL SURVIVOR STORY

By Leroy Allen

Leroy Allen

DEDICATION

I want to dedicate this book to my mother, Juanita Hayes Allen, a strong woman, for her love and undying devotion to me.

ACKNOWLEDGEMENT

First and foremost, I would like to give thanks to the BIG MAN above, GOD, for putting me on a path of understanding and giving me the wisdom to have compassion for others. And giving me the foresight to make intelligent decisions in my life, Good Orderly Decisions.

To my father, Charles Walker, for sharing his teatime wisdom with me. To my uncles, Roger "Bud" Walker, Mathew "Matt" Walker, Conrad "Connie" Barmer, Russell "RC" Barmer, my influential mentors and for showing me patience, guidance, and giving me my foundation for a business sense. My brothers and sisters Marvin, Leslie, and Michael for showing me love, Charlene, Starr, and Candy for sharing the laughter and sorrow. Thanks to Sterling Walker, my first cousin, who has stuck by my side through ups and downs. To my sons, Troy and Cory Allen, the light of my life. To my grandsons, Joshua, and Koreland that holds a special place in my heart. To Mr. Buggy Smothers who stood by me through the good and tough times during my mentorship, friends who have inspired me, and help push me forward toward my goals and those who have offered their prayers. May you find my story an inspiration to reach your 'light at the end of the tunnel.' May the divine light shine on you, empowering you to reach your fullest potential.

INTRODUCTION

Unlike most television crime shows, <u>The Wire</u>, created by David Simon, was a fictional portrayal but neatly introduced Baltimore City to the world throughout an entire season. A city of corruption, unsolved homicide and drug cases, a police department under a federal consent decree, and a city official caught with her hands in the cookie jar, leaving fewer funds for the citizens. My reason for writing this book is to show the world that there are two sides to Baltimore City. My side is a real survivor story, and how I achieved my dreams and goals despite being faced with problems and social stigmatization.

Leroy Allen

TABLE OF CONTENTS

CHAPTER 1
CHILD BORN TO ADVERSITY

On a cold kitchen floor, a young 22-year-old woman name Juanita Allen screamed in pain as she was about to give birth. Earlier, she had called for a midwife and her mother to help. Back in the 1950s, rarely did a woman in an impoverished state go to the hospital to give birth. Many families could not afford health insurance to pay for doctor and hospital visits. When it came to childbirth, you would call a midwife to assist with the delivery of a baby.

After the birth, there were times a decision was made to abandon the baby. It was not unusual for an unwanted baby to be dropped off on a church or hospital steps or placed in dumpsters; this may seem extreme and cold. You never knew the circumstances or the reason; it was no different in our household. My grandmother, Elsie, wanted to put me in the trash can but my mother wasn't having it.

My mother was inexperienced in these matters and needed to take immediate action. Elsie started taking charge and demanded my mother to put me in the trash, disposing of me like garbage. My mother looked down at me crying on the blanket at 1003 Cherry Hill Rd. and sees my older brother Leslie glancing at me. She notices proud brotherly love beaming from his face; there was no way at that moment, she was putting me into a trash can.

Leslie watched the midwife pull me out of my mother's womb and cut the umbilical cord that connected our mother and me. Leslie witnessed a life-changing phenomenon and became a true big brother in all aspects of my life. Leslie played a significant role in not only saving my life that day but became a protector of his small baby brother. He exposed me to many vulnerabilities that I would eventually face. Leslie and I had a unique relationship.

When I became a man, my mother explained to me why my grandmother felt it was so detrimental for her to keep a baby by another man that was not her husband. During those times in Cherry Hill it was a rarity to be married to a good man, and a reliable provider for the family.

Juanita was a beautiful red-boned black woman in Baltimore. Her husband, David Allen, was a truck driver and frequently traveled throughout the United States. His job kept him away from home and his family, but he kept food on the table. David and Juanita befriended Charles Walker and his wife, Gladys. Charles and David were working for the same company, only different shifts.

My Mother wanted to 'protect' the family's image, so listed David Allen as the father on my birth certificate whom she was married to at the time. My biological father was not revealed to me until I was nine years old. If my delivery had been in a hospital, my mother would've had put my biological father's name on the birth certificate, that man was Charles Walker. My mother had three sons by David Allen before I was born: Marvin was the oldest, then Leslie, and Michael, then me, the youngest.

My mother never discussed if there was a preconceived intention between the three of them, Charles, David & Juanita, about what to do with me. David became very suspicious of my mother after my birth. He began clocking her every move and whereabouts, and I could feel the ice-cold chill in the house when my mother and David were around each other. He would start an argument with my mother in a loud voice, telling her she couldn't appreciate a responsible man in her life and home. David said that these issues extended from my mother's childhood. I felt caught in the middle of a dangerous situation which my mother put us in. She made a tough decision in the marriage and then expected her husband to accept another man's child. My mother told David she was tired of protecting me from his verbal abuse. When I was about eight years old, she asked him to leave the house and never come back. That was the very last time I ever saw David and my mother together in the same house.

I knew my mother suffered a considerable amount of heartache because of the verbal abuse from her husband, and the combined lies and broken promises from my biological father. My mother endured a lot of stress created by the birth of a child outside of her marriage and a husband who felt he deserved better from his wife. As time went on David's disgrace became too overwhelming and the stress started showing on his face. You could see the anger in his eyes and feel the tension in his voice when he talked to my mother. The tension was so thick in the house; you could cut it with a knife.

My mother didn't know that her actions would start a domino effect because my brothers looked at me as the cause for their father leaving the home. I believe that's when their resentment towards me started. I think my mother just grew out of love with David but I'm sure she did love him at one time.

Growing up in this environment I always felt unwanted and a deep sense of guilt along with regret in my heart. I tried to figure out what was my mother's motivation for having me. One day she looked at me with a sincere heart and told me that I was her love baby regardless of her reasons for having me. I will always be indebted and thankful she brought me into the world under incredible circumstances.

I believe children that grow up with absentee parents and raised in a dysfunctional household need to be heard. They need a lot of attention to understand their feelings and scars that are so deep. The wounds you cannot see with the visible eye and can't be touched on the surface.

My mother loved when I would get her little porcelain figurines so I would pick them up for her from the store on my way home. I liked to surprise her every chance I got. She would put the figurines on the wooden shelf I made her in woodshop at school.

There was a gentleman in my neighborhood when we lived at 1003 Cherry Hill Rd. we called Mr. Buggy. He would take a group of (six) boys to caddy at the Suburban golf course in Pikesville, Maryland on weekends for extra pocket change. Mr. Buggy showed us boys leadership skills by taking the time out of his work schedule to build character in us. Not once did I feel different from the other kids and he would call me "Smiley". He allowed me the opportunities to build up my self-esteem and gave me a sense of self-worth.

Living in South Baltimore close to the harbor allowed my brothers, Leslie, Michael, and myself to bond. We would go crabbing early in the morning at about 4:00 am. Marvin would never go with us, it was too much of a dirty job, but he loved eating the crabs. Also, living close to the water gave me an appreciation and a sense of peace, although we were still in the hood. If you sit down close to a body of water, you can feel the calmness. Leslie taught me how to swim; unfortunately, that wasn't the case with my brother Marvin, who not only didn't like to do any activities with us but also often didn't want to have anything to do with me. He would torment me when we were young because he said he would always be the smartest one in the family and become a lawyer or doctor.

Well, as far as I can see, nothing has changed; he's still that dreamer.

Marvin looked upon me as being an outcast and not wanted. Maybe perhaps it was because I look different from the rest of my brothers, or simply because I was just the youngest. Either way, it wasn't a pleasant experience. Maybe this was a sibling rivalry between us, Marvin, and Michael being so hostile towards me even during the good times. I didn't like the way they treated me, so as a means of retaliation, I would urinate in their shoes before I went to school as payback.

My brothers use to call me 'Bee Dee Beat' because of my hair and 'Blackberry' because I would go blackberry picking by the railroad tracks. Leslie would put grease in my hair and brush it down good. He would say I looked as cute as a button for five minutes. Minutes later, after walking out the door, my hair would look like a mini Afro, as if it had never been combed.

One afternoon my mother told Leslie to get me ready because she had plans to take me somewhere special. She wanted me to walk with her to the Cherry Hill shopping center to get a few items from the grocery store. When we arrived, I noticed a man standing near the entrance. He waved, and my mother motioned for him to come to us. Mother bent over to me and said, "Leroy, I know you may not understand what I am about to say to you, but this man is your biological father."

While she felt I was ready to meet the man who was my birth father, I didn't even know what that word biological meant. I was just eight years old, and all I knew was David Allen was my father. Even to this day, I do not recall calling him father or any of my brothers calling him Dad, Pop or Father.

There I stood, astonished when this man walked over and introduced himself as Charles Walker, my father. Never had I felt such a sense of joy and pain all at once. His first gaze at me was a bit awkward. He looked me up and down and said, "He's not my son; he's too ugly." I was speechless and in shock; those words left a lasting impression. I looked at my mother and saw the shock in her face. I felt the pain in my mother's heart, a feeling of hurt, as a son would never forget.

For him to react the way he did and say what he said, I then understood why I never knew him up to that time, and why my mother felt it was best for David Allen to raise me as his child. There was no remorse in his voice, and no love shown in his eyes. "How dare you say something like that in front of this boy?" Mother grabbed my hand and swung me around away from him as I looked over my shoulder at him. We left Mr. Walker standing there by himself. There was a sense of smugness about him. As far as I was concerned, the man meant nothing.

I had a very puzzled look on my face when I asked my mother, "What's up with this guy?" She told me that it is a long story and one day we'd talk about it. "I will tell you all about my relationship with your father when you grow up. "But I want you to understand that at one point I loved that man." That's when I knew my mother had feelings for Charles and she felt I should try my very best to love him as well.

Charles Walker never made any effort to pay child support to my mother.

I made every effort to try to establish a relationship with Charles and perhaps to form a strong bond between father and son and thus grow to understand him. I wanted him to be that father I desperately needed in my life. There were many times when he could have shown me the love a son seeks from his father, but that never happened. Charles' efforts to be my father—while perhaps sincere in some respects—were futile at best. One Easter holiday, he stopped by in the morning and promised to come back with a chocolate Easter Bunny for me. I waited on the steps and the day became night, and excitement for the holiday turned to sadness. He never returned. My mother called me to come in the house. I was disappointed and so hurt I started to think that I was a mistake to be born.

After high school she met David, who was dependable, had a job, and would father three of her sons. David was a good man to my mother, but she was left alone a lot due to his career.

Like a tiger on the hunt, Charles knowingly approached Juanita when David was out on the road. Juanita was open prey. Charles used his savvy sweet talk and charming ways to seduce my mother into bed, thus creating me. His womanizing and lack of respect for my mother and responsibility for what he'd created, destroyed my mother's marriage to David. She cared deeply for David but was not in love with him.

As I entered my teens, the absence of a positive, strong, adult male in the household began to 'rear its ugly head.' I began to mix with the wrong people and began a life of mischief, trouble, and harmful activity. I became a bully and demanded that my classmates give me their lunch and lunch money. I would threaten all the kids to make sure they paid 10 cents dues or get beat up after school.

My brothers were just as bad, if not worse; if my brother Michael wanted something another kid had, he would take it. If they tried to resist or take it back from him, he would beat them up.

Bullying became standard, and I believe resulted directly from a lack of attention and love at home. My transgressions also included getting suspended from school consistently for fighting and looking under girls' dresses. Looking back and reflecting on those times, I was indeed up to no good. All I did was give my mother a severe headache. All the while, my so-called birth father would never step in and give me discipline and guidance that would've perhaps steered me in the right direction and away from the mean streets of South Baltimore. My father was always full of philosophy and sayings but never practiced what he preached. All this just showed me how to be a street thug.

Charles Walker came from a small town called Littleton in North Carolina, and he was a smooth-talking hustler. He loved his purple 1965 Chevy Impala convertible. My dad would cruise around the neighborhood, shoes shined, pressed shirt and trousers, looking sharp. He would promise you the world and give you nothing in return; it was a practice I became very familiar with. It's was clear how he seduced my mother. My mother was vulnerable to his charismatic charm; that is how he became my father.

My father was the 'jack of all trades and master of none.' Every day was a new adventure or a get rich quick scheme. One day my father called my mother and asked her would it be okay to take me on a trip to North Carolina to meet some of his family members. My mother thought it was an excellent idea for me to get an opportunity to meet family members from my father's side.

It was a very long ride from Baltimore to North Carolina, but when we arrived, the family greeted me with open arms. During my visit, I soon learned my father's family had their share of 'issues' too. Initially, the Walker family was from Canton, Ohio, but my grandfather, whom they called Papa's was from North Carolina.

When I arrived, my cousins told me that my Uncle Mac killed Papa because he came home drunk one evening and started beating on his wife, Mary Tom, my grandmother. The story was, Charles and Uncle Mac shouted upstairs, "Papa, take your hands off of mama!" Papa came running downstairs with a knife in hand, and he cut Charles and then Uncle Mac. He said, 'I should kill you both for interfering in my business!'

Meantime, Uncle Bud came into the house with a gun. Charles and Uncle Mac started screaming, "SHOOT Papa, he is going to kill us!" Uncle Bud froze in his shoes, and then he said, "I CAN'T kill Papa!". Uncle Mac rushed over to Uncle Bud, took the gun and shot his father one time into the chest. They rushed Papa to the hospital, but he died. After the death of Papa, it broke Mary Tom's heart, and she never recovered from the death of her husband. No mother wants to see her child placed in a position that makes them feel that it is necessary to kill their father to save her life.

Visiting the south put me into an environment that was completely different from the one I was experiencing in Baltimore City. I learned how to feed farm animals which required a firm commitment to work on a farm. One day I asked my cousin Claire Belle, "Where I could go to get a cold soda?" She said to me, "We can walk over yonder and get a pop." I asked her, "What do yonder mean? "She said, "It is just a short walking distance." She said maybe it's about a mile or so; in the city a short walk means two or three blocks. I honestly had a great time down in North Carolina meeting my father family members.

CHAPTER 2
MY CHILDHOOD

The oldest of three, my mother was a child herself. A native of West Baltimore, she had her first child at age 17, and within about 30 months, Juanita gave birth to three children. I was her fourth son. As a young mother, Juanita did not closely monitor her children's whereabouts. She spent a considerable amount of her time working as a nurse's aide to support her family and attended church functions.

When you are being raised by a young single adult, there are times when you will find yourself in an adult situation **and** making adult decisions.

When we went to school, there was never enough to eat, so we went hungry a lot. We never had stylist clothes like the other kids, but at least they were clean. On school mornings, you'd roll out of bed from a late-night and go to the kitchen and pour yourself some cereal, not caring about what you were going to wear. The roaches in the kitchen were so bold, they would run up the wall and across the ceiling, and sometimes they'd fall off the wall into your cereal. All you could do is shake your head and ask yourself, "Do I deserve this? There has to be a better life." I would pluck the roach out of the cereal and pour the milk if we had any and eat it. Sometimes there wasn't anything else to eat, so there was no wasting of food.

I was fiercely protective of my mother. As an adult, I came to realize my mother was searching for herself. She was a very nurturing woman who lacked the education, skills, and discipline to provide for her family.

Leslie took me under his wing from the day I was born. He was not only my big brother but my protector and teacher too. Leslie always seemed to know when I was going to get a spanking and would stand in my place. My mother didn't mind as long as Leslie wanted to take my spanking.

I recall one hot summer day we went swimming across the tracks. There was a construction site that contain a man-made water hole. But in reality, it was a mud hole. Mom permitted us to go but told my brothers, "DO NOT let Leroy get muddy. Under no circumstances are you to let him get into the mud." So off we went to the water hole, I didn't know how to swim so Leslie was going to teach me. Someone pushed me into the mud which was the kind that gripped you and held you tight. When you moved, it sucked you in more. I screamed for help. Leslie dived in the mud hole and pulled me up on the bank. They waited for the mud to dry and my mother to go to work before they took me home. When we got home, they gave me a bath and put the muddy clothes in the laundry bag. The next day my mother decided to do laundry and found the muddy clothes. She asked whose clothes are these, I said mine. She asked me what happen, and I told her Leslie and Michael took me to the mud hole and threw me in.

She asked them who pushed me in, nobody said anything. They both got a beating. I didn't get a beaten, but they never allowed me to hang out with them anymore, not even crabbing or black berry picking.

I grew up in a dysfunctional family with very little adult supervision. There was never anyone around to discipline me when I was doing wrong. No one wanted to give me the necessary love and attention to put me on the right track to be successful in life. I had no choice but to grow up fast in the streets of Cherry Hill where I found acceptance and nurturing at a young age. I found myself exposed to male figures, both good and bad; but rarely a positive role model.

I assumed the responsibilities of my older brothers because they lacked the motivation to help our mother out in her times of need.

We lived across the street from the city dump, and I realized it held a lot of opportunities, but the big challenge was a lot of rats. Rats struck fear and uncertainty in my heart and mind. Wow, those vicious rats brought a fight for my survival. But hunger overrode my fear. I knew that discarded food from the grocery stores was sent straight to the city landfill along with old wooden pallets. Pushing past the fear in my gut, I faced those rats every day. They not only challenge my basic instinct for survival, but they were also my competitors. I learned how to maneuver around those rats. I got very creative just by getting up at the crack of dawn, which allowed me to stake out the right spot to get what I needed and roll out to avoid any fighting with those vermin. One day at the dump, I came across some new wood that would be great to build a shoeshine box.

My new venture of shining shoes would allow me to feed myself and to be my boss. It excited me to be my own boss. This gave me a feeling of great pride and accomplishment. After building my box, I set up my new shoeshine stand by the Greyhound and Trailways stations in downtown Baltimore City. I would catch people going in and out of the station, seeking out those with the dustiest shoes. I would holler out in the crowd, "Hey! Get your shine over here 50 cents for one person 75 cents for two people!" Through experience, I learned that the most traffic was in the food court so that I would post up my stand there. For sure I would be there Saturday and Sunday no later than 9:00 am and would go home around midnight on weekends, tired and exhausted. I would still get up and go to school on Monday morning.

The following week, I ventured back to the dump, looking for some more wood and came across an old broken-down wagon. It needed some serious fixing up; precisely, it required a long screw to go in the middle of the wooden tongue and a wooden crossbar. I engineered it by attaching a heavy rope on each end of the crossbar with wheels, which allowed me to pull and guide my wagon.   After fixing the wagon, it became a working wagon for me.

This wasn't a toy in my eyes, a practical resource that empowered me to start my second little business. I started working five days a week after school, standing outside our neighborhood supermarket, asking people to carry their packages home. My rate was 50 cents downhill and 75 cents up any hill. I lived in a community called Cherry Hill, a location where everything is within walking distance but a reputation of being a violent place.

My mother's high school sweetheart and first love was Raymond Branch. Being he was her first love; she gave him her most valuable gift, her heart. But Raymond loved his liquor more than my mother. When Raymond got liquored up, he got mean. Sometimes, my mother got in his face to calm him down and she'd paid the price by getting a beat down. I still have bad memories of Raymond and my mother in battle. She fought back, turning the house upside down and in disarray. The furniture tossed around, and things thrown to the floor. After seeing that, I felt so sad for my mother and felt so helpless at the same time because I couldn't protect my mother from being abused. It left a scar of guilt on my soul. My mother with her face completely swollen from Raymond's brutal beating, called my uncles (her brothers) RC & Connie to come to her defense.

They came over and gave Raymond an old-fashioned beat down. And while holding him down, my mother took her revenge out on him by hitting him in the head with an iron. My uncles then dragged Raymond outside to sleep it off, closing the door behind him. The next day my mother changed the locks.

About a week later, while playing outside, Raymond approached me and tried to 'check-up' on my mother in hopes of reconciliation. He asked me to go upstairs and see if my mother would talk to him. Raymond wanted to apologize for what happened because of being drunk. My mother said she was not interested in what he had to say. Raymond started talking to me.
He told me how much he loved my mother. He talked about how things were between them when they were in high school and that she was his first love, and I knew my mother loved him.

I asked Raymond, "How can you hurt someone that you say you love?" He told me, "I can't find a job, no home of my own, and I can't support myself, let alone anyone else." "I'm no good, so I had a few."

Raymond's internal battle that he fought made him vulnerable to drinking heavily and hurting the people he loved, my mother being the first and foremost the victim of his rage. When he told me this, I had a lot of mixed feelings. There was a part of me that wanted to kill Raymond for putting his hands on my mother. In my heart I knew I didn't ever want to be anything like this man.

That day I made a promised to God if another man ever put his hands on my mother that man would never see the light of day. I also knew that I never wanted to be like Raymond, a drunk, and a failure. Perhaps if you feel as if you are a loser, then you are a loser, and you have lost half of the battle.

When my mother was able, she moved us to Seagull Avenue, away from Raymond. Nine months after we moved to Seagull Avenue his life came to an abrupt and tragic end. I'll never forget the day my mother got a knock on the door; the Baltimore City Police asked my mother to identify Raymond's body. He got into a fight and was stabbed to death.

One day I was playing outside on a hot day and came into the house to get some water and heard my mother crying in her room. I went to see what was going on, and why was she crying. "Mom, why are you crying?" I asked. Reaching out to me, she touched my cheek, tears streamed down her face, voice shaking, "Leroy, some days are sad ones. You sweet boy, you are just too young to understand". Chasing me outside, she said, "Go play!"

With age, I did begin to understand what was going on. My mother wanted to explain to me but couldn't at the time that she had made a lot of mistakes in her life. But I understood my mother better then she knew. I was her son. I felt more like a friend to my mother, and she had reached a crossroad in her life. She doubted herself as a mother. Only having a ninth-grade education, Juanita wondered how she could get a job to establish a safe home for her boys and daughter with no qualifying level of education.

She made choices in hopes of giving my siblings and me a better life than she had. My mother was looking for love in all the wrong places. While she consciously knew her decisions were not good, she was not able to come up with long-term solutions to deal with issues that affected her and her children.

I've always believed my mother wanted to be the best parent she could be, but she didn't know how. Unfortunately, her insecurities started long before I was born, back when she was a little girl by not knowing her biological father. She never met the man, which can be extremely difficult for a little girl growing up.

The void felt in Juanita's life created a hole in her heart, which encourage her to seek men with shortcomings and insecurities. My mother was looking for the consummation of herself and trying to find what was missing in her life.

It's tough for a young woman to balance raising small children and fulfilling a need to be loved by a man.

I wanted to be that male strength in my mother's life. I wanted the opportunity to show my mother that all men are not bad. Yes, I may have been a young boy, but I knew the difference between a responsible man and a player. I did not want to disappoint her and wanted her to know I would always be there for her. Even possibly restoring her faith and trust in men collectively.

Being the youngest of four boys, the family had a pecking order and I always had to deal with that thought. I was ridiculed for my shortcomings, such as wetting the bed and not being 'man enough' in comparison to my older brothers. However, I came to understand how important it was to give my mother the love, respect, and support she desperately needed in her life. I realized love was a missing part of her life. My big brothers never seemed to grasp it. My brothers Marvin and Leslie got so engrossed in trying to impress people at their school, especially Marvin, that we were not poor. Marvin was just downright ashamed of his family because of where we had to live. We did not have the most stylist clothes to make an impression. It was clear to me that my brother would instead fake it than to step up to the plate to help our mother when she needed it. They did not even attempt to get a part-time job to help out.   My brothers hurt me with their attitude towards our mother. I felt that since my brothers were older than me, they would take on some responsibilities in the house. After all, we lived in the same house together.

With no man at home to support our family and dwindling job prospects, my mother was forced to seek Social Services. She received welfare assistance for food and small monthly stipends. Once a month, my mother would ask one of her sons to go down to Greenmount Avenue to stand in line and pick up the welfare food. The food consisted of basically powdered milk, flour, cheese, and beef with gravy in a can. This food assistance seemed like it was never enough for all of us, considering we were growing boys.

My older brothers made it very clear to my mother that they would never pick up the food. Yet that was the food we all ate in the house. They feared being tease by their classmates if seen picking up food and rather than have food in their stomachs. I was the one pretty much designated to do the chores around the house for my mother.

On one occasion, my mother sent me to the grocery store with a five-dollar bill to get a few items for her. When I went across a parking lot, I notice some older boys who looked up to no good. No sooner than my thought came to be real, they shouted at me and told me to come where they were standing. I took off running as they ran after me for about two or three blocks, they knock me to the ground and tried to take my mother's money. I fought the bullies off the best I could, but it was two against one. When I returned home, the scars of my battle were evident with a bloody nose and a swollen eye. My mother scolded me, telling me to "always pay attention to your surroundings when you go outside." I didn't fully understand why I was to 'blame.' I took it as a lesson learned, and I told my mother at the end of the day, I may have gotten bruised and battered, but I still had her five dollars.

The other thing I realized early in my life; pride does not put food on the table. I learned that lesson from my oldest brothers. As I grew older and more mature, my mother relied on me much more because I was a son that she could depend on. My trips to the grocery store became a more frequent occurrence as well as going to the welfare department to pick up the food.

Being raised in 'the hood,' it was all about surviving from day to day; it could be a dangerous place to live. I always had to be aware of who approached me and not take anyone at face value.

One day while I was on one of those runs to the store for my mother, I heard a noise, "POP! POP! POP!" It scared me. I had never heard a sound like that before. I saw a lot of people running towards the corner where the sound of gunshots came from. On the ground was a beautiful woman suffering from gunshot wounds to her body. I saw a big ugly man hovering over top of her. He stood there and just kept on shooting the gun until it was empty. You could hear the sound of the empty gun, click, click, click. That was the very first time in my life I had ever seen a woman shot and murdered. I was screaming for help. I was stunned by this occurrence and it changed my life.

The police officers came running over to arrest the man with their guns drawn, and hands shaking with fear. I think the police officers were just as surprised as everyone else standing around watching. I could see the fear in the officer's face and eyes as they wrestled the man to the ground and handcuffed him. I ran home crying. Why would somebody want to do that to another person? I felt terrible and sad for the woman. I told my mother what happened and how the lady was screaming out for help as the man kept shooting her. Mother comforted me. She held me close and dried my tears because I was distraught and confused. Once again, my mother reinforced her knowledge of the street and told me to, be aware of your surroundings. Needless to say, after seeing the death of that pretty lady on the sidewalk I had no problem understanding what my mother was trying to teach me.

I felt if I were big enough with body mass, I would have jumped on that man and beat the living daylights out of him. It is one thing to disrespect a woman, but it's a sin to take someone's life because you allow your emotions and insecurities to control your mind. That's not a real man but a madman who's out of control.

After witnessing the violence in my own home, my mother abused by a man she thought she loved, left a lot of mixed feelings and emotional scars that still have not fully healed.

I've always felt protective of women; at an early age, I learned my mother was a victim of men who lacked self-esteem. In my heart, I wanted to protect my mother by whatever means so she wouldn't have to endure this type of abuse from anyone.

My cousin Sterling (my father's brother Matthew's son) received a lot of respect from Charles for being such a good student. We'd get together, and I observed the respect my father showed to Sterling for going to school and being an excellent student. I learned early in life how to mature fast, be responsible, and be able to resolve problems quickly in a constructive manner to make things better.

I will always remember and always appreciate the woman who nurtured me when I could not nurture myself. The woman who changed my wet diaper, fed me when I was hungry, who nursed me back to health when I was sick, who dried my tears away when I was sad, and who told me that there was no ghost in my bedroom waiting for me after I turned my lights off. You should show your mother appreciation now because you can never turn back the hands of time. I love you, Mother.

CHAPTER 3
I BECAME A MAN

After we moved to Seagull Avenue, my mother started looking for and found another church to join because she was disappointed with the old church rules and congregation. Also, it gave my mother a fresh start, leaving a lot of bad memories. She felt being around innovated and positive people would give us all more positive opportunities.

When we went to the old church, my mother was always looking for inner peace; and at the new church it seemed to me she found that inner peace. After joining the new church my mother began listening to gospel music seven days a week, clapping her hands when certain songs came on the radio or the television, thus creating a more positive environment.

She no longer allowed anyone to drink around her children nor verbally or physically abuse her. My mother started to show no tolerance for any negative behavior around the house, even though she still drank a little from time to time, and smoked cigarettes.

Because my mother was on public assistance, she thought if she joins the right church her family would get the support they needed to have a relatively comfortable lives because of the church's generosity, especially during the holidays. She was soon to find out that was incorrect because only certain churches will provide for their congregation. At times, my mother would ask Social Services to upgrade her food coupons because what we were receiving each month just wasn't enough food.

Mother ask the pastor of the old church if he would introduce her to other churches in the area where she could get some assistance. The pastor advised my mother to contact the Department Social Services and maybe that was her reason for leaving his church. My mother had already submitted information to the Department of Social Services to request an increase but never heard anything back.

The pastor from the new church asked my mother would she be interested in sending her sons to the Big Brother Mentoring Program in Baltimore City. My mother was hopeful that a mentor relationship with a positive adult male role model would have a positive impact on her sons' life. At least this is what she explained to the pastor.

I believe during those years mother wanted us in a new social program that built character in children, especially unruly children that stayed out in the street all hours in the night. I think the old pastor had other things on his mind towards my mother. On one occasion, an old guy from the church picked us up from home in a church van, took us over to the community center to play some pinball and basketball. After the community center close, we went outside to wait for the church van to pick us up. It started to get late then started to rain. We couldn't believe that the old guy didn't come back to get us and left us standing in the rain. He never notified my mother of our whereabouts; the church had my mother thinking that we had run away. But we were not that type of bad kids to run away from home. I was young, but I understood when the system was jerking my mother around.

She always wanted us to have a better life. Mother didn't know how she was going to accomplish that mission, but she believed family values started in the church. Maybe the real reason the local church wanted us to be a part of their 'family' was to help keep their mortgage paid not to enrich us spiritually and provide the community support. I learned communication skills within the church. After seeing my mother get rejected so many times, I quickly learn to separate my needs from my wants.

My mother couldn't have been prouder of me when she would come home after out looking for employment and find some food on the table or in the refrigerator.

One day, my mother came in the house and said she felt it was time for her to take charge of her life. She gave her heart and soul to God and with the will of God she would be focusing on how to please him, not man. She said that God would never reject humans needs and wants. After praying for some years, she finally got a job as a nurse's aide at John Hopkins Hospital in Baltimore, Maryland.

We were very young when so much transition came in our life. She found this new Pentecostal church with a new pastor. I think there were five or six churches in Cherry Hill within a five-minute walk, but she wanted nothing to do with them. I would never question my mother about what she felt we needed in terms of spiritual nourishment that brings wisdom and understanding and guide us through life.

It would take so long to get to church; we would fall asleep on the bus and miss our stop. Sometimes my brothers and I would get on the bus and get off downtown to play pinball at the arcade and hang out until it was time for us to go back home.

One Sunday, Michael and I did our typical Sunday 'routine,' and when we returned home my mother asked us what the sermon was about that day. We were caught off-guard and had no answer for her. Michael and I punishment were, to read the Bible every Sunday when we came home from church. We read the Bible to my mother until she was satisfied. We understood the words we read but not the meaning. She then told us to stop ducking church on Sunday.

No doubt, mother was like no other. She felt that just because a building is constructed, it does not mean that it is a house of God that can build a strong family structure through worship. What I never understood about my mother is she why she sent money whenever she could spare it to the TV evangelists, one in particular, Reverend Ike. Reverend Ike always seemed to capture my mother's attention and money. Every Sunday from high noon to 3:00 pm, he would deliver his 'gospel.' He would ask all 'good Christians' to donate 10% of their earnings to his 'mission.' My mother didn't have a lot of money. Between her little welfare check and the money she made working as a nurse's aide at John Hopkins Hospital allowed her to give money, which she couldn't afford.

I will always wonder why she would send her last dollar to those pastors with multimillion-dollar churches. why she failed to 'see the light.' I showed her a passage in the Bible, where Jesus spoke of false prophecy: Matthews 7:15-23. The apostles instructed believers to be diligent in faith and understanding of Christian teaching to discern false prophets when they arise. Yet some evangelists and pastors own Rolls-Royce automobiles, live in two mansions, and have private airplanes. But there were never enough funds in the church to help Christians that may require some assistance.

My mother continued taking us back to the same church and the same preacher every Sunday, hoping she would receive a blessing from the church. I didn't get suspicious of God, but I got very wary of what the church or pastor's mission. Most of the sermons preached were about obtaining freedom and being free. The Bible is a source of strength and is needed today to give people hope.

In black communities across America, every Sunday, thousands and thousands of us go to church. At times we act as if we are at a fashion show and worrying about who's driving the most expensive automobile, who has the prettiest wife, or who has the most handsome husband. It's as if many of us go to serve our purposes and not that of God. Corruption and deceit run more churches today than ever before, take a look around.

The concept of stewardship in biblical terms started in the beginning with Adam and Eve; they immediately understood that God is the owner and provider of everything. Everyone and all things belong to God for his purposes. Responsibility was given to mankind to have domain over the earth, to care for it and manage it for His glory. That is what the bible means to me.

My mother instilled in me a strong spiritual foundation not made from brick and mortar but from God's word in order to stay focus on his path in life.

I learned a lot from the Bible by just taking the time to understand the book; I always knew that God is a good loving God. It is man who corrupts the house of God. A church is just a building symbolic of God, and He does not reside there. God is all around us, and He is everywhere we are.

CHAPTER 4
MY VIETNAM WAR EXPERIENCE

In 1969, the United States Army drafted me and sent me to Vietnam as a combat soldier where I experience trauma, fear for my life and looking death in the face.

The Vietnam War was one of America's costliest in terms of loss of life since the Civil War. Because of decisions made by President Lyndon B. Johnson, there have been a lot of movies, and stories told about the war in Vietnam. My account.

Because I was there, let the facts be known -- there were a lot of incompetent generals, and politicians were pressured by the public to end the war. Politicians were more concerned about getting re-elected rather than that America was on the wrong track by sending U.S. troops to die in a foreign country over a conflict that didn't concern us. They were not concerned that each soldier was given the proper equipment once they arrived in Vietnam to fight the war. A vast majority of the weapons, which were received by the soldiers, were faulty in some way. The M-16 would misfire or would not perform very well when it was wet, especially walking through rice paddies. Nearly 60,000 U.S. men and women lost their lives in the Vietnam War.

I was 17 years old when I got drafted and sent into combat. Jobs were very hard to find during the Vietnam war. Needing a source of income, I dropped out of high school. My thuggish behavior was at an all-time high. I was getting suspended so often in high school, and I spent more time in detention than in class. I began using drugs to numb the pain of being rejected all through my life by my family.

I wanted to catch my life before it got too far out of control. I needed a real job to keep me occupied and to provide for my mother. I came up with a plan to go to the US customhouse and register for my draft card to show proof that I was 18 years old, although I was only 17. No questions were asked, just sign on the dotted line, now I was 18 years old on paper, which enabled me to get a job. Yes, being 18 years old helped me to get a job. My draft card came in the mail classifying me as A-1, the fact that I lied didn't matter to me; I just wanted to work. But soon after, I realize there were consequences for me lying about my age. I worked for about six months, and then I received a letter in the mail from selective services. It indicated the date, time and the place to report for duty. My mother could have died right there on the spot after she opened the envelope. My mother was beside herself.

She asked, "Leroy, what have you got yourself into this time?" and why did I lie? "You are only 17 and had no right to commit fraud by signing your name to something when you knew good, and well, you are only 17 years old." I tried to explain to my mother no one wanted to give me a job unless I could show proof that I was 18 years old. It was the only way that I knew that I could get a job. I had to produce a selective service card, so I went and got one.

Fearing my mother was going to kill me, I just wanted her to understand that I needed a real job. I loved her so much and couldn't bear to see my mother going without. I explained to her that if I have a choice, I will give my life for her. I was a man now, and I made my decision to uphold my responsibilities around the house. I reminded her that her brother purchased a home under the G.I. bill, and I, too, could do the same for her.

She told me, "Leroy, how do you expect to survive in a war in the jungle? You're barely 75 pounds soaking wet! There is no good reason for you to go into the Army during wartime. I do not want a want house that bad. And if you don't make it back alive to me, that would kill me!" After a long and heated discussion, she decided that she was going to call the selective service office and straighten this mess out. But when my mother started talking to the United States customs officer, her face changed from straightening this situation out to a face showing concern. Whoever my mother was talking to on the other end of the phone, he or she said if your son signed the documents under the wrong pretense, it's not a mistake, it's a false statement. The only choices were to pay a $10,000 fine or ten years in jail or go to Vietnam. So I decided to take my chances in Vietnam.

I was scared to death once I received that induction notice. You heard about a lot of our soldiers killed in Vietnam. Then I got to thinking was I ready to die? Just before I had to report to Fort Holabird in Baltimore, I was hoping to get some idea of the war by going to a movie. During that time, it was a hit movie out called The Green Berets starring John Wayne, which I thought was very realistic. Boy was I a naïve 17-year-old. It did not hit me until I saw a little action and realize that the soldiers that were getting hit were not getting back up on their feet; this was the real deal. I went to Fort Bragg in North Carolina for basic training for four weeks. I was then sent to Fort Dix in New Jersey for AIT training for another four weeks.

AIT training is a specialized training which was to prepare soldiers for Vietnam, such as looking out for booby-traps and tunnel rats. There is not enough training to prepare you for combat. I had to learn how to survive once I got there in the jungles of Vietnam. Because there

27

were no jungles in Jersey, I couldn't benefit from the training. Maybe the Army should have sent me for training in a more wooded area in the country with unbearable heat. I didn't understand any of this, I was just a young punk from South Baltimore.

After training, I was sent to Oakland, California, to be shipped out to Vietnam on American Airlines. What a long flight. I went from the east coast to the west coast, then to Asia. Once the plane landed, and I walked off the plane the heat in Vietnam gave me a hot blast in my face. I have never felt that kind of intense heat in my life! I knew nothing about the Vietnamese people, the weather, or the terrain because I did not receive the proper training.

I was assigned to the First and Second Air Mobile Calvary Combat Division. I was issued all my military equipment such as my rucksack, my weapon, ammunition, and other essentials that would take me into combat.

Upon arriving I was welcomed by my company commander, and the platoon sergeant. The very first-day walking patrol in the jungle, a sniper took out our lead man, the point man, with a bullet in the head. The shot went through his helmet, and you could see his brains still beating in his helmet on the ground.

Talk about a 'wake up call'! I thought the jungle would be like a deeply wooded area like in the parks in the United States. Boy, was I wrong! The only way you could get around was by helicopter.

Monsoon season was coming upon us. If you have not been to South East Asia, it may rain for days or weeks, with a consistent torrential downpour. Awful for a combat soldier, rain and snow are the worst weather to fight in. It did not matter what weather came upon us; we were fighting in it.

Commanders wanted a high body count of the enemy, the more we kill the 'happier' the commanding officers were. The soldier who killed the most VCs would get ice cream and a cold soda. Walking through the water with the water buffalos next to you and with your weapon over your head, you are hoping and praying that a firefight doesn't break out because you are in the water and if your M-16 gets wet it will not fire. That meant you were undoubtedly a sitting duck.

I questioned the M-16 efficiency because it would jam a lot during the monsoon season. You would never think in a million years that your government would give a combat soldier a weapon that they are experimenting with, knowing that lives would be lost.

In the Vietnam War, a soldier would have to think for himself and go into a serious survival mode because you would be surrounded by booby-traps. We had to watch out for tunnel rats, that's an enemy soldier who lives in an underground tunnel, that waits for the enemy to pass his line of fire so he can kill as many as possible before they return fire, killing him.

You start asking yourself who will be the next to die amongst us. After being in a combat zone for six months, it wears on your mind and morale. On one occasion, my company commander asked me to go on a recon mission that I felt was unsafe, but I went anyway because it was an order.

Three other soldiers and I were sent deep in the jungle with no big guns and no helicopters to aid if we encounter the enemy in night fighting. We were on our own. No sooner when it was my turn to be on watch duty, with my night vision lens on, I saw nine or ten enemy soldiers at a distance from us, not close enough to walk into us. I asked myself should I engage the enemy by myself or alert the other three soldiers to allow them to help me fight the enemy. I wondered would the other three soldiers have enough time to gather their composure and find the enemy in the dark. I decided not to engage the enemy out of fear that the other three soldiers would wake up in disarray. It would have been just as dangerous for all of us, not knowing exactly where the enemy was, and which direction would have made us vulnerable. I let the enemy walk by without making a sound. I've always believed a good soldier is one who lives to tell the story, not dying in a senseless fight.

What the Captain did not understand at that time, I already had a lack of respect for authority from my childhood, and I was ready to explode and question his competency. Before drafted in the military, I would always question authority. I came from that generation. What I didn't know then was that the U.S. Government needed bodies to fight this war in Vietnam, a war where so many lives were lost.

To this day I believe the US government could not have cared less where you came from; the projects in the city, or from the small mom and pop farms. It just did not matter what color, or what creed you were, it was all about getting the bodies in the military to fight this war in Vietnam. Where I come from, the inner-city, to compete in a battle in the jungle was a significant change in my life, and to this day, I believe that some people in the US government wanted to utilize this war to get rid of the so-called undesirable generation of black and white. It is time to speak out about how the government was killing our youth on the battlefield.

The war was a disaster because of the lack of strategic planning and leadership. Many of the military officers didn't understand how to fight this jungle war. American politics has so many young men fighting and dying on the battlefield, and for what- American freedoms? During the late 1960s to the early 1970s, no one attacked America that I am aware of. I had to ask myself, what was America's interest in North Vietnam? To this day, I still do not know the answer to that question.

One thing I learned from that war, you can't force a man to fight a war with no real cause and with no threat towards his freedom in our country. I was the same age as the hippie generation in America that believed in free love and protested the war in Vietnam and rebelled against the system on most college campus around the country. If you graduated from high school or was a high school dropout, you received a draft card. It didn't matter if you were rich or poor, it was the duty of all male American citizens between the ages of 18 to 21 to report for duty. You were required to apply for a selective service card once you reached the age of 18 and obligated to serve in the military for two years. The draft is unheard of today because today's armed forces are voluntary. Many of these young men already had emotional and psychological issues and a lack of respect for authority before they entered the military. A considerable number of Vietnam veterans still have emotional and mental problems, along with addiction problems.

Most of these men are in their 60s and 70s and seek treatment at a VA hospital. They also file claims with the Veterans Administration to receive benefits because they have received injuries while doing their service in the military. The United States has more homeless veterans than any other country in the world. I believe there is no longer a draft because the psychological pressure of combat can lead to PTSD or suicide, which the United States military is dealing with these issues today.

Once on patrol, I fell into a bomb crater that was about 15 feet wide 9 feet deep. When I got out, my back was hurting. I explained to the commander that I needed x-rays. My commander said that is not going to happen. I need every man on the LZ to defend from the enemy. I told him I'm not at my best! Then he made a statement to me under his breath, calling me a northern black. In a moment, I was placed under arrest for disobeying a direct order and was ordered to go to the bunker. The Captain at that time took my M-16. I went into the bunker, which was surrounded by sandbags around midnight. After my weapon was taken, we got hit, it looked like the 4th of July, but the difference was instead of the fireworks going up into the air the fireworks were raining down on us. I truly felt hopeless and abandoned because I had no weapon to fight back to protect myself. My base commander didn't seem to care that the Captain took my M-16, leaving me nothing to defend myself. I went into the bunker to secure my safety. At that time, a fellow soldier from Chicago said "Brother Bmore, the best thing you can do now is smash yourself as close as you can to the hill and toss grenades over your head so no one can sneak up on you!"

I knew that I would be in the fight of my life; it seemed like the firefight was never going to end. 'Chicago' crawled over to me and said, "Brother Bmore, I don't think that we are going to make it, so can we pray together?" I said, "Brother, I am not going to play with God because only God has power over life and death. I would never have taken my chances on this battlefield to make a promise to God and break it because I'm afraid." I told Chicago it is with God to do as he sees fit with my life. "Chicago, he can give me purpose, or allow me to die here knowing that if I survive through this battle, I will be chasing Asian pussy in the village tomorrow!"

When the fighting concluded at the break of daylight, you could see all the bodies, dead bodies everywhere. For as long as I live, I will never forget that sight. Dismembered bodies, arms, legs, heads and other body parts lying around. Blood, blood, blood, and more blood; I don't care to mention any more here. The sounds of crying and moaning, many were lying there dying, crying for their mothers.

Most of us were only 18 and 19 years old. These visuals, I will never forget and will remember for the rest of my life. I was given the task of gathering up the dead soldiers and putting them in their body bags. We had to get them back to the base to be sent back home for proper burial. These mental scars are burned in my brain.

I got orders to report to the Base Commander's office because I disobeyed a direct order from my Captain. The Captain brought me up on court-martial charges. I could not believe what I was hearing, after fighting for months in this war; this is what I got in return. I was sad, anger and sicken but I used my time wisely by reading and listening to reports of the casualties we were suffering on the battlefield.

All old soldiers have war stories to tell, and I am no exception. The war of Vietnam was full of stress, senseless death, and one had to have a lot of faith to survive.

The battle of Thon La Chu (1968) Tat Offensive caught the US military by surprise, and the enemy soldiers captured the city of Hue. During this chaos, the cavalry was sent to save the Marines as the Army chopper of the 2nd Battalion /12th Calvary flew in the rescue mission to save the marines. The Army chopper landed close to an open rice paddy without any conventional artillery or air support backup, and we suffered considerable casualties.

The Vietnamese had a lot of soldiers, a high fighting position, and enough firepower to encircle the US marines. The marines had suffered 60% casualties, had no supplies, and little air support. The soldiers on the ground were fortunate to slip away at night and avoid detection.

Then there was the attack on Nui Ba Den. Hundreds of enemy soldiers launched a surprise assault on a poorly defended American base. The base was quickly overrun and burn to the ground. There were 24 Americans killed, 35 wounded, and some taken as prisoners of war. Most of the soldiers survived in bunkers or by fleeing the base. They hid in the mountains. Some referred to the battle as a massacre. Why? Because the attack was so sudden and so many soldiers had no rifles to defend themselves.

The American Generals made one final attempt to block the Ho Chi Minh Trail and found more enemy soldiers than expected. As the enemy assaulted remotely located Fire Support Base Ripcord, the Generals decided to evacuate the base. Four American battalions from the 3rd brigade, 101st division, conducted an aerial assault that lasted 23 days with the loss of at least 75 Americans, and 463 wounded.

Dozens of helicopters were shot down or damaged while many soldiers were left behind. Just a small piece of evidence that many battles were lost during the Vietnam War. There was more, but hiding embarrassing losses came to be standard procedure. Some commanders tried to spin that loss as a victory, but the loss of FSB Ripcord was hidden from the public until 1985, and the slaughter at Ho Bo Woods wasn't recognized until 2011. I always had my suspicions of the Army. They sent me to that 'meat grinder' without adequate training.

For my transgressions against my commanding officer, I was assigned a lawyer to defend my rights. The day of my court-martial, we went in front of a Grand Jury. My commanding officer, Captain Goldberg, started by first telling the court all the bad things about me-- that I was from the urban area and it was hard for me to get along with other soldiers. He took my weapon because I disobeyed a direct order to go out in the field when he told me.

My attorney, Lt. Johnson, was a young lieutenant from Boston and he asked the Captain to give a reasonable explanation to this court of why he took a soldier's weapon in a combat zone, when the Captain was aware of the enemies' proximity to this landing zone. At this point, you could hear a pin drop. The Colonials (four full bird colonials) asked the Captain, was this true, that he took my weapon in a combat zone. The Captain said yes without any explanation why he took my gun. The Colonials ruled that the Captain violated the code of conducting himself as officer. Taking a combat soldier weapon in combat cannot be tolerated under any circumstances, so what did the United States Army do? They let me go.

I was given a general discharge under honorable conditions for disobeying a direct order. At the end of my court-martial, a psychological evaluation should have been made due to combat stress. My mental state after my tour of duty was extremely fragile and volatile. The court ordered no evaluation at that time. I didn't understand the significance of this discharge. However, my lawyer explained to me that this was good. I would get full benefits and have a clean service record.

I did thank him and let him know I was very appreciative of him defending my rights in court. To the US Military Attorney, who represented me with service number US 67-005-615, I thank you!

American Airlines took me from Vietnam to Oakland, California. On my flight home, a flight attendant asked me why I didn't have any stripes on my uniform. I told her I'm just a combat soldier trained to stay alive. Then I told her, "You do have some heroes in the belly of this plane with stripes on their uniforms going home to families with a broken heart and not knowing what this war was about. I told the flight attendant I believe that America should only send soldiers to fight and die in situations where the USA is threatened.

After a small layover in Oakland, I boarded an American Airlines flight to Baltimore, where my young girlfriend picked me up. Naturally, she wanted to know all about my experience; I explained to her that I was bitter and very angry with the Army because I had no place to report, or follow up, no psychological counseling, and no rehab.

I came home from combat and experienced nothing but fear and stress after being surrounded by so much death. I was very shocked to come back from fighting for my life and then to see all the protesting of the war in Vietnam by people my age. Movie star Jane Fonda protesting took it to another level. She visited the enemy's camp and took photos, which allowed the enemy to think American citizens had one voice.

The total military personnel who served on active duty in Vietnam was 9,087,000 between the time of August 1964 and March 1973. Puerto Rican men were drafted to fight in the war even though they could not vote in presidential elections. Overall, blacks suffered greatly because 12.5% of the deaths in Vietnam were African American but they only made up 13.5% of the Army. Statistics states that 76% of the men sent to Vietnam came from lower/middle class working families.

CHAPTER 5
AFTER VIETNAM

Some people may say that I was lucky or blessed, coming home in one piece during wartime. If I had to describe my feelings coming back, it would be thankful to God, very fortunate and very lucky. I am still grateful to God even with the memories of all the carnage and destruction I witnessed up close. I felt depressed and did not have a deep appreciation for life after seeing so much death, an experience that will be forever embedded in my brain.

I got off the plane in Baltimore at Friendship Airport (now known as BWI Thurgood Marshall) on a hot July day in 1969. I had a girlfriend before I left to go to Vietnam; she came to pick me up at the airport. She had 'promised me' she would wait for me to come back home from the war.

I could tell there was something on her mind as we were riding back from the airport towards my mother's house in Cherry Hill. She explained to me that she met a new guy, and she fell in love with him while I was away because of the uncertainty of our relationship by me being in a war zone. Well, there is a common saying in the military that goes like this, 'Jody has got your girl and gone.' and I was no exception.

I accepted that fact. You can't control a person's feelings or actions; besides, I wasn't sure if I was going to return home alive. I thank her for picking me up at the airport and dropping me off at my mother's house.

We rolled up to my mother's house, and I ran through the open door and into the open arms of my mother, grandmother, and brothers. They were waiting for me. It was a great feeling being home so I could start a new life.

Considering all the money I sent home to my mother, not only was I excited to see my mother and family but more excited to get my hands on my money. Shortly after I walked in my mother's house, you could feel the cold breeze in the air, and there was something that just wasn't right. I was praying that she did not spend my money. All my dangerous combat pay plus regular pay was compiled together in each check. All the checks went to my mother while I was overseas.

I just knew in my heart that I had a considerable saving established. Then I learned that my mother spent my money. I was devastated and crushed. I felt betrayed and let down.

My grandmother was my mother's chief advisor; my mother explained to me she spent my money because they had a dream that I died in combat. Having not received any psychiatric care when I came home, I had nothing to hold me together, no glue, no meaning, no insight. I lost it because I didn't understand how anyone could take someone else money that's fighting in a war in the jungles every day for his life to come home to nothing.

My grandmother said God told her to tell her daughter what to do with the money. From that point on, I realize my mother was not too smart when handling another person's capital, and when influenced by her mother.

From that day on, my mother never held any of my money for any reason. I knew as a young boy my mother struggled with our daily household budget. I remember when she used to go back and forth to the pawnshop to make ends meet.

I moved in with my mother because I had no other place to go. For a while, I was hoping to find a job right away; instead, nothing turned up; I would've taken a janitor job.

I think what stopped me a lot from getting employment was most employers would ask guys like me, "are you just getting back from Vietnam"? I would say yes in a proud voice, not knowing that some Americans viewed Vietnam soldiers as 'Baby Killers'. What a gesture of disrespect to the soldiers that gave their lives and died on foreign soil to be called Baby Killers. What made matters worse was the government did not provide veterans with mental health evaluations coming back home after carrying a weapon 24 hours a day. You slept with it, and you had to keep it dry when you were in the rain. You woke up in the jungle searching for the enemy while knowing you're always being watched and shot at.

I needed rehabilitation after I returned from Viet Nam. The reality was quickly soaking in while living in the house with my mother, and I needed a job bad. It seemed to me she never had enough to pay her bills. My mother received an eviction notice, and if she didn't get some money right away, the rental agency would put my mother's furniture out on the street. I found out my mother already had a date to be set out in the street. Knowing she couldn't come up with the rent money by the due date, she explained to me that she would have to move in with her mother and stay there for a while until she could get back on her feet.

Mother felt I would be more than welcome to come with her until she got her place. I was packing my stuff up, getting ready to move with my mother to my grandmother's house. I saw a problem look on my mother's face, and she informed me that grandma Elsie did not want me to move into her home. I was only 20 years old, but the refusal of my grandmother to allow me to move in with her was a huge wake-up call for me. My mother came up with another plan.

Mother said she was going to call my oldest brother Marvin who didn't live that far from our house on Round Road. I believe my mother got into an in-depth conversation with my brother Marvin, but at the end of the day, I don't think my oldest brother's heart was really into helping me out. He told my mother it would not be a problem, and it would be okay for me to stay there for a while until I can find a job. My mother told me what Marvin said. I could see my mother got very excited because she did not want me to sleep on the street.

Marvin told my mother that I would need something to sleep on, so the only thing my mother had was an old plastic patio lounge chair for me to sleep on. Marvin and I moved the lounge chair in the center of the living room. Because the living room was the center of the house activity, I would go to sleep after the kids went to bed for the night. I'd leave early in the mornings to search for a job before my brother, and his kids got their day going.

Marvin had two young daughters and one son. One day I got the surprise of my life; Marvin came to me and asked me to leave. Marvin's wife had her way of thinking and didn't feel safe with me being around their daughters.

I called my father. I had to explain the situation with my mother and grandma Elsie, rejecting me, and what happened at my brother Marvin's house. I asked my father, "Why is it that nobody in my mother's family wanted to be around me, not even my brother?" Charles never answered my question, and he just said, " Leroy, as long as you need a place to live, it's here for you. "
He said it would be okay to stay with him. "Damn," I thought to myself, is this the same man who said he was my father now decided to act like a father? Hmm, it made me very suspicious of his motives, but that wasn't my biggest concern at the time. I needed a place to rest my head and find a job. He gave me a spot to sleep.

Moving in with my father was going to be tricky, and I knew I'd have to be very cautious. My father was a great manipulator with house rules or lessons to be learned in life; he called it.

Topics of conversation included how I was going to get a job, which put an awful lot of stress on me, especially after I came from Vietnam. Imagine you spent months, waking up with a rifle in your hand, drudging the jungles and swamps 24/7 and all of sudden you don't have that routine anymore or a sense of security, i.e., your rifle; which provided you that sense of protection.

Suddenly an overwhelming feeling of desperation overcame me as I looked across the kitchen table at my father while listening to his strategic advice.

CHAPTER 6
TEATIME LESSONS

We all can reflect on those moments when our guardians or parents shared their pearls of wisdom or as my father would say, "free lessons of life." Yes, while living with my father, I got a healthy dose of those Teatime Lessons. Charles had a routine: if you stayed with my father, you lived by my Charles' routine and his house rules period. One habit was each morning at 6:00 a.m. it was "Teatime" at the kitchen table.

One morning I watched Charles standing by the stove, teakettle whistling as he poured the hot water into cups to make us some tea. Turning from the stove, in a slow deliberate manner, Charles brought the cups to the kitchen table, and he sat across from me. I was about to head out to look for a job. Charles leaned in and looked at me calmly then stated, "Leroy, the best way to control your destiny is with a good woman."

Another of my father's pearls of wisdom – he once told me, "Leroy," he paused as to formulate his thoughts " Emotions drive women." Any man can catch a woman, but the name of the game is keeping the woman, and because you are my son, you are getting these lessons for free." He explained to me that a woman is control by her emotions, and men are controlled by their fear of failure.

One day we were driving past a cemetery, and my father asked me, "Do you think everybody in that cemetery died from natural causes?" I replied, "I don't know." He responded to me, "It's a lot of fools in that cemetery," which at the time I didn't understand. He meant that people put themselves there before their time by doing foolish things.

The next day he said he would give me a test on values, then he said, "when your young lady comes over the house tonight, I would like for you to use this kitchen napkin. After you make love to her, wipe her pussy and hold it for tomorrow morning I will then tell you what to do." And so, I did. The next day the lesson came. It started by going to the bank. My father fills out a deposit and a withdrawal slip. After the transaction, he handed the teller the transaction slips and asked me to give him the kitchen napkin. He gave the teller the napkin and asked for a withdrawal. The teller didn't seem to amuse with that joke, but my father said it wasn't a joke at all. "This is a lesson for the boy here." It was a statement that he wanted to make by showing me that pussy has no value. That had a devastating impact on my life, a lesson that tests values and loyalty. He said, "Women are like cars, some are like Mercedes-Benz, some like Cadillacs, some are like Volkswagens, and some are like Chevys, and then there are junkyard cars too. You can build from the number 0. But whatever you do in life, shoot for the moon in case you fall, you will surely hook a star on the way down." We had great conversations over the kitchen table doing teatime together. I was hoping that we would form a closer bond that healed our past rocky relationship.

One hot July day, a friend of mine named Randy and I was downtown hanging out. Randy ran into a couple of cutie pies that he used to go to school with, so he introduced me to them. These two young ladies were hot! Very fine and sexy. They made my blood race in my veins, both ladies had green eyes and long red hair. Hot! Hot! Hot!

In the '60s, my generation experimented with free
love and bucking the system. Baltimore was one of the
first cities in America to allow equal education and
segregation. I loved getting very fresh with the young
ladies of all races. I told the young ladies that I was living
with my father and he pretty much gave me the freedom
around the house. I asked if they'd be interested in
checking out my place. So they replied yes, and we got
on the bus, and went to my father's house. It was a plan
that everybody was down with, and we arrived at my
father's house at about 6:30 in the evening. I figured my
father was upstairs asleep when we walked in with the
young ladies. He quickly woke up after he heard us
coming in the door and hearing laughter from the ladies.
Charles yelled down the stairs to me, "What's going on
downstairs?" I replied, "Dad, you want to come down so I
can introduce you to some young ladies?" But he never
came down. I thought nothing would be said after I had
asked him to meet the girls. I just assumed he didn't care.
Then I took one of the young ladies to my bedroom, no
more than 15 minutes after being in my room, not enough
time to get out of my clothes, my father started shouting
out to me, "Leroy" in a loud voice from his room. "Leroy,"
he shouted, "I want to see you right now in my room."
In his voice, I knew something just wasn't right. Once I
got into his room, he looked at me and asked me what I
was doing, I thought, you're a man like you didn't know. I
said, "Randy introduced me to a cutie pie while we were
downtown hanging out with some friends. " Then, for
some reason, Charles asked out of the blue, "Are these
two young ladies white?" I guess he could hear their
voice; he became crazy mad. I thought he wanted to get
his groove on too.
I had to ask my father, "Does it make a difference what
color the women are?" Something inside made me start to
question the Charles Walker teachings. "I thought you

told me that all women were emotional, and pussy has no value."

But my father felt because he was born in the South during the Jim Crow era in the 1930s, you couldn't have sex with a white woman without being put in jail. Even if she consented or if she was your wife; you could still get locked up. It was so bad back then you could even get locked up if you stare too long at a white woman in the South. You could get a reckless eyeball charge that would also land you in jail.

I tried to explain to my father that we are from two different generations, but my father did not want to hear it. He yelled at me to go back to my room and tell one of the young ladies he wanted some pussy too. "Tell them if I am not going to get any pussy, there will be no fucking in this house. "Do you understand?"

You could have heard a feather hit the floor; it was so quiet throughout the house. I was shocked. It was one of those big shocking knockout punches he threw at me. Never, never in a million years did I see that one coming. My father was acting like a teenager, throwing a fit, wanting to have his way, and showing me no respect in the process. I was shell-shocked, and it was a lesson I would never forget.

I told Randy what he said, and he sympathized with me; he too felt shocked, and we both were going through this nightmare with my father. We explained the situation to the young ladies. We all agree it would be best for them to go home, and we apologized for my father's behavior. I called them a taxicab. While waiting for the taxi, one of the young ladies asked me, "Why did your father feel he needed to disrespect you and your friends in that manner?" I didn't have an answer for her. Charles' behavior seriously shocked me.

After the girls left the house and Randy went home, I went back into the house. Charles couldn't leave well enough alone. No, he started with his words of wisdom telling me that white women would do anything to please a man. But at that point, I found his words offensive. I turned and confronted Charles and said "a woman is a woman no matter what color she is. She is a nurturer by birth; this is what you taught me. Yes? " The anger started contorting his face. Charles did not like his own words, nor the fact I was repeating the lessons that he taught me. The moment became very tense because he did not get his way for the first time in my life. I was not going to subject those girls to Charles Walker.

I had witnessed pure unadulterated racism, saw the selfishness in my father's face, and heard it in his voice. Charles's profiling girls into a category, which was the total opposite of what my mother taught me about girls - 'love who loves you back.' It doesn't matter what color she is; all women want to experience joy, love, and happiness for a lifetime.

During this time, my father was working as a Merchant Marine, and he traveled around the world. I didn't know much about what he was up to. Then one day, he sat me down at teatime and said that he had a way of bringing African heroin home in drums on the ship he was traveling on.

Leaning across the table in a low voice, he asked me, "Leroy, do you know how to get rid of this?" What a surprise, coming from my father. Now I knew my father had some stuff about him, but I could not believe he wanted me to help him sell the drugs on the street. Grant it, I knew living with Charles had its conditions, but this? I knew nothing of the sort, but he didn't care. You do what you had to do; I can still hear his voice, "You still need to pay the rent."

Charles, with his master manipulator skills, kicked in, and he said to me, "Beg, borrow or steal; it doesn't matter. I expect you to pay. Because you are still a youth, you have to sell the heroin on the street for me." With me having to pay rent, needing a job, my mind raced, and I agreed to assist him. Neither Charles nor I knew nothing about the game which was played on the street. I knew Charles was putting us in serious jeopardy with this game of his.

Charles taking the lead, he contacted this man and told me to go meet him down at the hotel on North Avenue. He gave me a package to deliver. Once I gave the man the bag, a bunch of police rushed into the room and arrested me. They put handcuffs on me, put me in a squad car, and then went to arrest Charles. I had no idea what was going to happen.

During our trial, the judge indicated that my father was talking with a police informant as the buyer. The judge made it clear that he felt it was extremely shameful for a father to introduce such deliberate criminal behavior to his teenage son. But I was not left untouched by the incident. My father and I both were sentenced to 18 months in the Jessup Correctional Institution. The real irony of this is that my father and I was just two cellblocks away from each other. The lesson I learned from all this was never to get caught with your pants down, and I never trusted Charles again.

Yes, I was upset with my father, but I had to look at the big picture. I needed a roof over my head, and after all, I was only 20 years old. After six months of living with my father, I finally got a real job at the A&P bakery. All I wanted to do was save my money to get as far away as I possibly could from my father and get my own place.

This experience left me finding it hard to feel secure and trusting other people with my well-being. The harder I worked; I was able to feel more confident in my life. First, I put my faith and trust in God and myself to give me a better experience. God bless the child who has its own.

After working in the bakery for two months, I met a young lady that had a car and lived with her father. She was a young lady named Sandy that had three small children, and I was far from ready to be anybody's father.

Although she was older than me by two years, I was 20, we got very close, and had a unique connection which developed into a committed relationship.

One day Sandy called me, sounding very distraught. She informed me that she was pregnant with our baby, which was terrible news to me because my life just a wreck. I could not assume any more responsibilities. With disbelief in her voice she said "Leroy, I thought it would be a nice surprise for you, and I dropped by your father's place and informed him of my good news." Her voice was cracking with emotion, "only to discover you weren't home. Your father asked if he could give you a message." Her voice was heavy with emotion, but she continued, "Charles told me Leroy that I wasn't the only one you have sex with…"

When she told me that, it surprised me too, that my father wouldn't show any emotions whatsoever to the news. Sandy was telling my Dad she was pregnant by his son, but Charles's 'pearls of wisdom' and being 'the master of manipulation' he had other intentions with the information she was giving him.

Sandy was distraught to learn that I was two-timing her. Then Charles saw this as an opportunity to add salt to an open wound; he made a pass at her by inviting her into his bedroom; 'let a real man make love to you. No 'real man' acts in that kind of manner toward a woman, at any age for any reason.

All I could do at the moment was explained to her the kind of relationship my father and I had. At least as far as I was concerned, that Charles's lack of respect for what's appropriate was to be expected and not to trust him. Charles was Charles; his actions didn't make the things he did or say, right in my view.

That evening I approached Charles and asked him, "What justification did you have for acting in such a disgraceful manner towards me?" Charles responded by going up the stairs to his room. I heard him moving around, and he came back down the steps. The next thing I remember is Charles pointing a 30-30 rifle in my face, yelling at me, "I brought you into the world, and I can take you out. I will take you back to the earth myself". It was crazy and surprised me that this man never bought me a pair shoes but felt that he had the right to take my life over a woman pregnant with my child and insult me as a man and as his son. Once again, he spat out words with so much venom that he was ashamed of having his blood in my veins.

Charles was so angry with me for questioning him about his disgraceful actions. My Uncle Mac felt he had to intervene before Charles pull the trigger. Uncle Mac told me to leave the house, and he gave me a $20 bill out of his pocket and said, 'May God be with you. '

God was with me that day. It became painfully clear that the man who brought me into this world was selfish, inconsiderate, cold, and unremorseful. I left, walking out with the little things I owned, fitting in an A&P brown paper bag.

My relationship with both my father and Sandy was in ruin; once again, I was starting from scratch. I was sitting at the bus stop weighing my options. I heard a female voice, "Leroy, why do you look so sad?" I was surprised by her calling my name. I looked up to find a female friend named Shirley from my high school days.

"Hey, Shirley, nice to see you!" "It's been a minute." Shirley sat down next to me, and I proceeded to tell her what happened with my father in his house earlier. I told her I got kicked out and that I had no place to go. "Leroy, I got a place off Park Heights on Queensberry. You can catch the bus with me and stay for a while." Shirley was living in the northwest section of Baltimore City, which was a long ride on the bus. She explained to me that she was separated from her husband and had two sons. She looked at me and stated that I was more than welcome to sleep on the sofa.

I was still working at the A&P when I moved in with Shirley, but it was a 2-hour commute each way to and from work. I needed a job that would be closer to Shirley's place. Every so often, I'd see Sandy. Then one day she approached me at the bakery, she said, "Leroy, sorry your dad kicked you out like that. It's not right and entirely my fault. I should have never gone to the house." Sandy apologizes to me.

I told her, "there's been bad blood between my father and me since the day I came into the world. It's not your fault". Charles is just crazy." She said, "Leroy, I lost the baby. I had a miscarriage." it was unfortunate but also relieving because I knew that I was not in a position to take care of a baby. Nonetheless, two months later, I quit my job at the bakery because I couldn't handle that long commute.

I started to look for work since I moved in with Shirley closer to where we lived. It was just a matter of time before we were sharing a bed and became a couple. Two years, in and out of jobs, Shirley got pregnant.

Reflecting now, it never dawned on me to think that my first-born son was an illegitimate child, like his father and history repeating itself. Shirley was still married to another man with two biological sons, and my son became precisely like his father. My son was product of his environment, born from lust with a mother and father living in nonproductive climate, continuing a cycle that had not been broken.

As time passed, my transgressions would come back to haunt me. My oldest son Troy told me when he got older that I was never there to show him or his mother love. The love and devotion he and she needed so badly in his life but never got, and he hated me for it. He was too young to understand and it was not his job too. I should have been a better father to him. I honestly did my best to be there for him.

While I couldn't be there for him like I wanted, I made sure I did all I could for Shirley and her sons, Mark and Damon. During Christmas, knowing kids would be expecting gifts, I would buy somethings for him and his two brothers. I would also made sure when school started that the boys got what they needed for school. I would do my best to make sure my son and his brothers had clean and neat clothes, as my mother taught me. It would have been wrong for me only to buy my son the things he wanted for Christmas and needed for school and not buy for the other children.

We decided to move back to Cherry Hill so that I could get a job working at one of the chemical companies in the area. What I did not realize or understand at that time, Shirley and I brought the children back to the same environment where we were trying for so many years to get away from.

I found a job with Davison Chemical Company in Fairfield. Day in day out, it was the same work, loading chemical into a mixer. I got into a job rut because there were no benefits and no raise and to top it off I was getting bored very fast. I felt stuck. I couldn't even afford a car, and I had to depend on a coworker for a ride or the bus to get to work. I felt at that time in my life I had to get on my feet. I was trying to make a bad situation into a positive one and turn it into my advantage.

During the 18 months I was in jail with my father, we were surrounded by career criminals with self-motivated intentions. Many times, you do your time and come home to a struggle. The events I was exposed to, like Charles' manipulation of me, and being thrust into circumstances beyond my control, I started to think like a career criminal. I began to think I can do much better than Charles.

I needed a car but lack credit so I asked my mother if she would sign for me. She said yes and I got my first car, a 1971 VW beetle. The car allowed me to move around

51

and meet new people. I needed to make some fast money, so I asked my brother Marvin if he knew how to reach an old school mate, Doc Crosby. Doc Crosby lived behind Giles Road in Cherry Hill and we would see him when we visited our grandmother Elsie. I admired him because he was able to leave Cherry Hill and build a better life for himself. He was always dressed real sharp, drove a fancy car and had a lot of pretty women. He owned a convenient store on Carrollton Avenue in West Baltimore. About three days later my brother took me to his store. Doc took me to the back of the store and showed me how the drugs were package, the different sizes of packages, and told me where to go in New York to pick up more supplies (drugs). He also gave me a gun, I asked him what the gun was for and he explained it was for my protection. I took the gun but really didn't understand. I told him I was ready to make some real money and was tired of making mistakes. He sat me down and explained to me how the 'game' is played and how to make money. I learned how to use a scale, how to package it, how to distribute it in the street and how to manage workers.

We worked out of the pool hall in Cherry Hill. I gave strict instructions not to bring anyone to my house. One day one of my workers, Al, came to my house. I looked out of the peep hole and saw Al and someone else that I did not recognized. I assumed he was a friend of Al and opened the door. The stranger bust in the door, pushing Al inside. I ran into the bedroom and got my gun. He announced that this was a robbery. I looked around the corner and saw him standing over Shirley and my son Troy with a gun in the dining room. Immediately I shot him, and Shirley and Troy dropped under the dining room table for protection. He then shot two rounds into the dining room table, missing Shirley and Troy. I shot him one more time and he shot two rounds back at me, hitting the bedroom wall. I tried to shoot him again, but my gun jammed. Another accomplice waiting in the getaway car heard the shots and came in the house and pulled his friend out. He slammed the door behind him; Al got up off the floor and was walking toward the door to open it. I yelled to Al not to open the door and at that moment the accomplice shot through the door, hitting Al in his chest. Al was explaining to me that he thought he knew the gunman and that's why he brought them to my house. I notice Al was bleeding and asked him if he knew he was shot. He did not realize he had been hit, he said, "shot where". I said, "in your chest" and he asked me to take him to the emergency room because he did not want to die.

I went outside to find someone to take him to the emergency room while I waited for the Police. A classmate name Bird that Al and I went to school with came down the street in his brand-new Thunderbird. I waived him down and asked him to take Al to the emergency room because someone tried to rob me, and Al got shot. Al came out of the house bleeding from his chest and Bird said, "hell no, I don't want any blood in my new car". Eventually, I convinced Bird to take Al to the hospital after giving him a blanket to cover his seats.

My brother Michael lived across the street and came over to check on me. The robber's gun was laying on the floor and I asked Michael to take my gun to his house before the Police arrived in case they searched my house.

The Police came and asked me what happen. I explained that a guy knocked on my door and asked for a glass of cold water, it was a hot July day. When I open the door, he announced that this is a robbery. I told them we started tousling for the gun. I told the Police I shot him twice with his gun and he dropped the gun and ran into a waiting car. The Police immediately issued an APB for a black male in his early twenties that maybe suffering from a gunshot wound. He received a response that a black make just came into University of Maryland Hospital with two gunshot wounds to the abdomen. The Police asked if I could give a positive ID. I said yes, and they drove me to University of Maryland Hospital. They took me to the sixth-floor operating room and ask me to look through the window to see if I could identify him. I said I could not see so they dress me in a sanitary gown and mask and took me into the OR to get a closer look. I already knew he was the shooter, but I wanted to get close enough to bang him in the mouth. I got a couple of good hits before the doctor order the Police to remove me from the OR. I felt he disrespected me and my family.

Six months later I received a letter from the robber from jail. He apologized and told me his trial was coming up soon and he was looking at 10 years for attempted robbery. I wrote back that I would not show up in court and I hope you learn a lesson from the two hot ones I put in him.

This started me on a path of selling drugs for the next 15 years of my life. I was pretty successful until the DEA end that fast and dangerous lifestyle.

CHAPTER 7
STREET SMARTS/SURVIVAL

One of the most basic human instincts in life is survival. A challenge that started the very day, I came out of my mother's womb. Born in the ghetto, some call it the hood, raised in poverty, you are bound to face a life of hardship; you find yourself in the fight of your life. Surrounded by death and violence I grew up forced to navigate my life around dangerous situations. I taught myself by trial and error how not to get killed on the streets of Baltimore City.

For years, Baltimore City has been ranked as one of the most dangerous cities in America. I made my mind up long-ago I was not going to become a murder victim.

I had a plan early in life to provide for myself and my mother. I clearly understood survival is the most basic instinct of all. One must use that instinct when they are struggling and to overcome fear. Use your dreams as a major driving force to take you to another level and to flourish. Excellence is never an accident but is a result of being focus and never giving up on your goals and dreams.

The use of wisdom and the choices we make in life from many alternatives are not by chance. Determine your destiny. Nothing stops the man who desires to achieve. Every obstacle is simply a lesson to develop one's achievement and strengthening an individual's accomplishments.

Being forced to work and do your best, will help you to develop self-control, self-restraint, will power, contentment, and happiness. To mention a few of the virtues which the idle person will never experience.

We all may encounter hardships while here on earth, but it's not about the difficulty, it's about how we survive and what we learned from the struggle. One solution I used and continue to use is discipline. When tough times come my way, I think of my basic needs such as food, shelter and clothing, and the care of those I love.

We all get motivated for different reasons in life, even when we are confronted with tragedy. I know it takes courage sometimes in life when you must take a chance on yourself. Do not be afraid to take on any risks that will improve your experience. We all have a precious gift called life. When a circumstance or a turn of events change in your life, right or wrong, you and you alone must accept the change and adjust accordingly.

I learned early in my life that pride does not put food on the table, a lesson learned from my oldest brothers. As I grew older and more mature, I became 'the reliable' son to my mother, much more than my brothers. She could depend on me. My situation and demeanor played a significant part in my life. It was about me giving my best and having to step up to the plate and be counted when needed. This is the time when most people's survival skills and techniques kick in.

We are all different, yes, how we approach and confront our struggles in life when it comes to dealing with hardship. There is one thing we all can agree on; doing nothing will get you absolutely nothing.

My survival came out of desperation to fight for a better life and a way out of the ghetto. To make Baltimore City streets work for me using my knowledge as a golden rule.

1I once heard, "Some days are just bad days, that's all." You must experience sadness to know happiness.

When I'm fighting to make a better life for myself, I remind myself that not every day is going to be a good day, that's just the way it is!

I must admit it's hard when you have nothing to make something worthwhile in your life, and there's no one to teach or mentor you. No role model on television to show you. No father or father figure to take you by the hand. When life comes crashing down on you, you realize you are on your own. Sometimes the bad things that happen in our lives put us on the path to the best things that will ever happen to us.

One of the best things that could happen to us is when we learn how to turn that disadvantage into an advantage. I believe children that grew up with absentee parents and raised in a dysfunctional household need to be heard, need a lot of attention to understand their scars that are so deep. The wounds you cannot see with the visible eye. That goes for anyone who became the adult in the house when they were just a child.

My mother was an extremely emotional woman; just watching a romantic movie would sometimes bring tears to her eyes. She loved receiving pretty things, so I would surprise and bring her a gift when I did well with my wagon or my shoeshine box. She loved it, and I love seeing her smile. She would like those little porcelain figurines I brought her on my way home. She would put the dolls on a wooden shelf I made for her in junior high school. I loved surprising my mother every chance I got.

Now your circumstances may be different from mine, but your future is in your own hands, and you should take the responsibility to create a comfortable life for yourself. My advice is to seek out knowledge and wisdom to enhance your experience while allowing your mind to adventure out the box. Focus on positive things that will improve the condition in your life. Apply these methods to your goals and let hard-work and planning be your driving forces.

Think about this! Would you walk down a dark hallway with no batteries in a flashlight? No. That is dangerous, your life is like a flashlight, and your common sense is your batteries. Always have a pathway and a plan when you are in the dark, looking for a way out.

My life-altering moment came when I witness my mother crying, which broke my heart, but I was only nine years old. I didn't understand why she was crying, but she explained to me that at the end of the day, there just wasn't enough food on the table and in the refrigerator to feed her four boys. She was sad that all her sons had was hand-me-down shoes and clothes. But despite growing up around poverty and violence, it never stopped me from striving to make a big difference in my family's financial situation.

Despite that the Department of Social Services provided our family with spam, powdered milk, and cheese, we still went to sleep hungry. It is hard to study or go to school when you are hungry and other kids making fun of you being needy.

My mother would buy good quality clothes and shoes so that they would last longer and could be passed down. When I received the hand me down clothes and shoes from my brothers, they would be on their last legs. So, I would make do with what I was given, but some of the shoes had holes in the bottom before I got them. Being innovative, I would just put some cardboard in the bottom and use a plastic bag to cover my shoes when it would rain or snow.

I've witnessed a lot in my childhood, my youth, and adult life. My experiences served to enable me to survive in urban America today and help shape the man I am today. There are a lot of people in the world that are book smart, have an Ivy League education but still will not have the common sense and intelligence needed to survive in the street.

A classroom doesn't give you the wisdom needed to navigate a dangerous neighborhood. I want to share with you some of my experiences in hopes that those of you who have gone through similar situations or have yet to deal with such a case, can use as a guide and learn something from my experience.

Whenever you're in the hood, you should NEVER appear to be lost, confused, or ask someone for directions. Most, if not all, inner-city areas are arranged in a grid, so knowing some things as simple as to look for the nearest highway. The safest thing you can do would be to find a fire station or hospital and asked for directions. There are some neighborhoods where you might not find a safe haven, or you might discover shady characters inside the service stations or convenience stores. If your gut is telling you something is wrong, follow your gut and don't take chances. Just get out, and don't hesitate. A person should never go into unfamiliar neighborhoods in the city without a full tank of gas. Always make sure you have a full tank of gas. If you are using public transportation, learn everything you can about the system. Familiarize yourself with the bus and train routes, and what time the last bus or train leaves an area you're not familiar with. Also, avoid wearing expensive or flashy clothing so you won't draw attention to yourself. This is not the time or place to look glamorous/sexy/unique.

In some places, specific colors, like excessive red or blue, are associated with gangs. If you are a woman, the best advice is don't look sexy or don't try to look pretty. Yes, it is a shame that you should have to suppress your individuality today, but let's face it, singularity draws attention. That's not something you want in a dangerous neighborhood.

Always be alert at dangerous locations and interactions. For instance, if you are in a grocery store and a very intoxicated person bursts in, yelling and waving a fist, what do you do? If you are street smart, you would casually go about your business making your way out of the store without drawing any attention on yourself. Someone who's not street lively, they might stare, confront the person, or even try to help the person by being a good Samaritan, this action may get you killed.

Those of you who may be visiting a big city coming from a small town should be very aware of your surroundings. Eye contact can be very tricky. If you are walking towards a person or a group of people who are checking you out or your companion, it's 'ok' to walk in the same direction, avoid eye contact. Don't make it visible if you walk directly across the street after seeing them coming towards you, but if you do make eye contact with someone, don't look away suddenly; shift your connection away slowly. At the same time, you don't want to hold a conversation too long, and this might invite a confrontation; always be alert.

You can be in a public place without making it evident that you are uncomfortable with your surroundings. If someone says something friendly, be polite but be brief. If you walk past someone who asks how your day is going, you can acknowledge them by nodding in their direction or reply with, "I am doing great, how about yourself?"

Some people are genuine and sincere, but as I've already said, always be aware. Women should especially be very aware of these kinds of situations. If you do encounter a threat, I would advise you to try to stay calm and not look afraid. Try to survey your surroundings; try to find help by notifying law enforcement. One thing that can be of tremendous help is to memorize the features of anyone who may try to attack you. If the person has a gun, most times, all they want is your wallet or valuables. By all means, give it to them, do not try to be a hero; your life is more valuable. When the criminal leaves, call 911 immediately.

Someone who is a street-smart person has a lot of common sense and knows what's going on in the world.

This person understands every type of person and how to act around them. A street person knows all the current trends in the streets and can adapt to different environments. A street-smart person doesn't pay attention to frivolous activity or conversation.

Avoid 'player haters'; these are people who come up with a reason to dislike you because of your success or something you have.

People who are well educated should not be categorized as lacking common sense, and those who are street smart should not be labeled as unintelligent. There are many types of people in the world who are hood-smart, not so intelligent, but are calm, crazy, wild, and fun to be around. Whatever the case, just remember that to survive in any type of environment, apply common sense, respect, and be aware of your surroundings always.

My confidence came to me at an early age when my mother brought a pair of barber clippers for the house so we could use them to cut our hair and perhaps make some money on the side. When I had an opportunity to cut someone's hair, I was able to observe a person's behavior and sometimes observe how people carry themselves in public. This allowed me to build my confidence and learn how to hustle by cutting hair in the neighborhood, maintain my poise, and learn how to make eye contact in a non-intimidating way.

You must understand what I'm saying: you don't always have to be in a classroom to get an 'education.' But don't use this as an excuse to drop out of school. Go to school; take advantage of your opportunity to get a free education. In today's world, a good education can carry you a long way in life. Also, get into the habit of incorporating God into your everyday life. Faith is a powerful and universal survival tool. You need to trust that God or a higher power has a plan and will look after you. HE will guide you through difficult times.

If you listen to what God is trying to tell you, your path in life will be a smooth one. In a crisis, faith will give you remarkable power and confidence to prevail in the face of adversity. You should believe that no matter how bad life gets, everything will turn out for the best. Be able to maintain confidence that your wishes and desire. Be an upbeat person who turns negative feelings into positive thoughts and understands that you have the power to endure in the darkest times and tough situations.

Always keep your dreams and passion for life. It will give you the inspiration and power to persevere in the face of incredible adversity. Still, be determined and focused on realizing your dreams no matter what obstacles you encounter. Life is a gift, and you should always make the most of it.

The key has the drive and willingness to devote yourself to a worthy cause. Having tenacity is the 'superglue' that keeps you healthy in tough times, as well. Sure, life hurts sometimes, but you can handle the pain and keep on going and know that love conquers all.

Your bond with family and friends should be unbreakable and give you reasons to live. When someone who loves you and depends on you, do your all not to let them down. Having experienced this in my life more times than I care to mention, I truly understand the importance of bonds.

In a crisis, your willingness to help others can be a compelling way to help yourself. Be compassionate enough to help others stricken by misfortune and what you can to reduce their suffering. Don't resort to selfish means of survival; be willing to think of others first. It is essential to use your mind positively by learning and thinking of how to solve problems. Intelligence can be a powerful tool against adversity, as well. Be able to anticipate and examine issues from various perspectives and find a realistic solution quickly. Learn to apply acquired knowledge from other situations to overcome immediate challenges.

Learn how to improvise, be innovative, and keep your spirit healthy. Have the mental ability to be steadfast and relentless. Master the art of staying cool and calm when others around you panic. When facing a crisis, a person's real character is revealed. Being able to have an innate sense of how to resolve problems or conflicts is what separates you from others. Your gut feelings come naturally and automatically to you, trust yourself to do what's necessary. Your responsibility for your life and your ultimate success depends on the choices you make in life.

CHAPTER 8
I BECAME A HUSBAND

My life came to a drastic change when I got married. I was introduced to my wife by a friend of my brother Leslie name Belinda. Her girlfriend, Pat worked for United Airlines as a flight attendant and seemed like a very nice young lady.

I had some problems in Baltimore with the DEA shortly after I met Pat, so I went on the run, jumping my bail. I decided to go to LA and start a new life. I drove to the West Coast and got an apartment at 1776 N Sycamore, behind the Chinese theater. At that time, the only funds that I had in my possession were about $10,000. I started a janitorial company with my brother Marvin's brother- in- law, James, which didn't do very well. While in LA, I had a lot of time on my hand, so I would hit the night clubs. There was a famous club I enjoyed visiting on Sunset Blvd call the 909 club. It was a great place to meet people, and I would go there often. The West Coast crowd had a different style in how they approached people than the East Coast; or should I say that the West Coast folks are more friendly and open.

One day, I was in club 909, and I see the young lady Pat that I met back in Baltimore. I decided to go over and strike up a conversation with her. I asked her what she was doing in LA. She said she worked for an airline, and this was one of her routes, LAX to BWI. I don't think she was too particular about getting involved with me, at that time but we became great friends.

As time went by, we reach the point where we wanted to spend more time with each other. She invited me to her place for Thanksgiving dinner in Baltimore. I accepted the invitation and flew to Baltimore. The next day before she left for work, I informed her that I had a few friends that were coming over her apartment. She gave me strict instructions not to allow any of my friends to do anything illegal in her apartment. I gave her my word, and no sooner than she left, I called Bobby Brown. Bobby was my old friend, I use to hang out with on the corners and pool halls in Cherry Hill.

I called Bobby Brown, a trusted friend because we started hustling together back in the 80s when we were young thugs on the corner. I found some excellent stuff that I picked up in LA, and I wanted to show him how he could make money in Baltimore.

I brought the goods back on the plane from LA to BWI; this took place before the 911 attacks in New York City. Airline security wasn't as tight as it is today on planes. I explain to Bobby I had something for him to test and to let me know what he thought about it. Bobby came over and spent the night, and I thought about what the girl said about having drugs in her house. I decided to take the drugs outside and bury them in the dirt. Around 4'oclock in the morning, the door got kicked in by the DEA. All hell broke loose. Little did I know that Bobby Brown was an informant and brought the police straight to my door. The entire time that I was in LA, Bobby Brown was an informant. After they kicked the door down, there were no drugs found in her apartment. They locked me up for jumping bail. I got out on bail again and was released to the custody of my mother, I went back to LA to get my personal affairs in order.

Because my life was in such disarray Pat though maybe she could be that missing link in my life. We could become closer if she showed me that she was willing to stand by my side in my time of need. Then out of the blue, she asked me what you think about getting married. She told me, "Leroy, you know that spouse and family fly free." She said that if we got married, it would allow me to travel around the world. It would also give me an education beyond what I could ever learn in the street. She said traveling would give me a chance to interact with people from different cultures and have different experiences in life. It would only enlighten me as a man and as an individual. I jumped at the opportunity, and we got married, but I still had federal charges pending for drug possession.

No sooner than a year after we got married, I went to federal court. She stood by my side when that day came, and I received 15 years: 10 years sentence and five years of special parole, which would allow me to participate in a federal program. It was probably one of my darkest days; when you are incarcerated, you have no friends, and you cannot be with your family. You are in a vulnerable position because you know that your family needs you physically, mentally, and financially and you cannot be there. You must ask yourself, 'how did I get into this situation.' But society says that you need to go to jail because you broke the law.

While I was incarcerated, I studied to become a dental technician. When I got out of jail, my wife and I resume a healthy relationship, but I was still bored. The money was coming in but was not enough for the lifestyle I liked. I asked my wife if she knew any friends in Los Angeles, Chicago, or anywhere that could assist me with where I needed to go to enhance my lifestyle.

After leaving the federal penitentiary I was sent to the federal Camp Center in Petersburg, Virginia. At the Camp Center, I could take up to a 4-day furlough. I ask my wife to get me a ticket so that I could meet this guy in LA she felt that I could become good friends with. We flew to LA and met a gentleman named Simone. He came to pick me up at the airport in a Rolls Royce convertible. I was so surprised and very impressed, and I knew that this man was about money. When he picked me up from the airport, I notice the plush carpet on the floor of the car, and the panels were just magnificent. On the way to his house, we drove along Pacific Coast Highway 101, where we stopped, and I decided to jump in the ocean in all my clothes. It was a good day for me because it was a fun day, and it made me feel free.

The next day I had no clothes to wear, so Simone took me to Beverly Hills and brought me a pretty good outfit. That was the first time that I was exposed to REAL illegal money, but it seemed he didn't take it seriously because cash was just a game to him. I returned to the Camp Center in Petersburg Virginia to check in because my furlough was over. I felt as though I accomplished my mission because, as they say in the drug world, 'I got a connection.'

When I was released, I went back to Baltimore and picked up where I left off in the drug game. Only this time, I was a little bigger because I had my connection, which was entirely on the west coast, and they had much better-quality products. Simone and I became terrific friends.

I learned a lot of things from Simone. He also had a broom manufacturing company where he ordered the straw from Cuba, and the wood handles in America where he put the brooms together with a machine. He promised to ship me a truckload of brooms to Baltimore so that I could start my broom business, LA Distributors. He kept his promise. I would have a product to be sold to provide clothes and keep food on the table when the drug game was slow.

I went to my uncle Bud to see if he would assist me in finding a location or warehouse for the brooms. He allowed me to use one of his offices. I started in a small office that my uncle rented on Reisterstown Rd in

Baltimore, MD. I started selling my brooms to small supermarkets, and this allowed me to accumulate enough money to purchase chemicals to sell retail. I could sell the industrial chemicals much faster than the brooms because they were repeat orders. I stopped going to California for a while because I was making money. I felt financially comfortable, and I was still in the game, but not as much as I was in the beginning. I would go back and forth to LA to place orders for my brooms as well as to pick up a 'package.'

I notice that Simone was getting high too much on his supply, which I was always told never get high on your supply if you want to make money. I started to get a little worried about Simone, and he would call me now and then and tell me that he was paranoid. He thought that people were coming to get him, so a lot of times, I would catch a flight to LA to see my friend. Not for business, only to comfort him, but it seems the more and more he continued to get high and paranoid. I stopped going to LA for about 3 or 4 months, and then I got a call that my friend Simone got locked up. While he was incarcerated, I tried to reach out by sending him some letters to let him know that I was thinking about him. Later I was told he was there for a short time before he died of an aneurism.

After four years of pondering what to do with my life, I decided to open an oriental furniture store in Silver Spring, Maryland. I would travel to Hong Kong to buy Asian furniture to stock the store. I stayed there for two years, but then realized the area was not keen on a black man selling oriental furniture. I decided to relocate to Baltimore.

My first son's mother and I struggled with parental rights issues. This conflict inspired my wife to have a child of her own. Only it wasn't that easy for her to get pregnant. She began to monitor her ovulation cycle. The doctor told her the only way for her to get pregnant was to have sex during ovulation. I would get calls from her saying, "Leroy, I'm ovulating." This meant I dropped what I was doing to rush home to impregnate Pat. There is nothing romantic about getting one of those calls: no passion, no lust, just performance on demand. But Pat wanted a baby, and as her husband, I felt obligated to give her that baby.

Eventually, she got pregnant, and we had a son named Cory. The day I laid eyes on him, I loved him. I love both of my sons and sorry I missed out on so much with Troy. Troy eventually worked at LA Distributors as a salesman, and it afforded us time to get to know each other.

Life was good, but Pat being an airline stewardess and raising a baby was a challenge. Because of her coming and going and my dealing and running a business we hit a brick wall. My life started to spiral downward, caused by addiction and guilt. My wife and I decided to file for divorce, and that left me on my own, which lead to my demise.

I started bringing people over to my house, which did not mean me any good whatsoever. It seemed to me something was lost in my soul. One day I could not take any more of the misery, the deception, and the loneliness. I laid across my bed, and I asked God, would you please show me the right direction so that I may please you. I wept as I humbled myself to God. God heard me, and he took everything from me that was illegally gained.

I sold my house, and I realized I had nowhere to go. I had lots of friends but only a few that I could trust, but it was one lady that I felt was honest and loyal and really had my back and was indeed a friend. It was Sandy, and she came to help me put my furniture in storage, and I stayed with her for 2 or 3 days. I knew that the DEA was watching me, so I did not want to bring any unnecessary attention to her doorstep, so I found another place to stay.

The DEA was relentless in their efforts to put me back behind bars. They located me at my new address, and I was getting ready to go jogging when I got a phone call from a gentleman that I had never heard before. He asked if he was speaking to Leroy, and immediately, I knew that it was the DEA, so I start flushing everything down the toilet. My girlfriend, at the time, was Audrey. Audrey and my little boy Corey were in the apartment when they kicked in the door. They picked me up and threw me to the floor and told me, "Leroy Brown, you are going downtown."

I was driven to Delaware and put on a private plane and flown to Oklahoma, where I had a parole hearing for violations, and they found me guilty of a preponderance of the evidence. I was sentenced to 7 years for violating my parole. Within those seven years, I indeed found myself, and this allowed me to reconnect with God. There were two books that I would read every day and every night, *The Millionaire Mind* and the *Holy Bible*. While reading the Bible, I came to understand that I wanted to do things to help people.

CHAPTER 9
SPIRITUAL AWARENESS

My spiritual awakening was a profound revelation in my life. It felt like a boost of power that transformed my mind, body, and soul instantly. It occurred when I was about seven years old. I awoke from my sleep, rolled over in my bed and felt something drawing me to look out of the window where I saw a white cloud in the sky. It was a stunning vision of a cross with a crystal blue background.

It excited me so much I ran and woke my mother up and told her to come. Grabbing her hand, I pulled her to my room. We stood looking out the window, and I pointed out where the cross was in the sky. I was shocked when she said that she couldn't see it. "Why not?" I asked. She told me maybe it's not meant for her to see, and that God works in mysterious ways. But because my mother was so religious, I thought for sure she'd know what that meant and why I saw that cross in the sky. After she went back to her room and not being satisfied with her answer, I woke my brothers up to see if I was going crazy. They too also said they saw nothing. That day I was amazed looking up in the sky and seeing that cross and know that it was a definite sign.

I believe a person should seek knowledge and understand the true meaning of spiritual awakening; I think it's a divine path to guide you to find wisdom and understanding and to allow your body and mind to receive spiritual food. It all starts with appreciating who you are and everything around you.

Each one of us keeps hope in our hearts and faith in our minds. Understand that no one is perfect, so don't look for perfection from any man or woman because we are all born of sin. We should learn from our past experiences in life to improve our future growth.

Experiencing a profound spiritual awakening allows one to enable himself to see how God can empower them to have free will of choice. This happen when I was in Vietnam, facing death. I felt HIS presence around me that made me feel safe. My faith grew stronger which allowed me to be true to my higher power. Your spirit will allow you to feel a unique sensation in your mind when someone is around you who is up to no good towards you. This may sound weird or crazy to some but is real when you receive and allow spiritual fulfillment to give your life purpose.

The biblical teachings I was taught as a child came in handy and is very enlightening as an adult as I learn about God and faith.

Many times, during the battle in Vietnam, I believe that there was a reason my life was spared. I genuinely feel that God has placed me on a divine path, a calling for my life, to serve and show others the divine wisdom of God, as taught in the Bible. Jesus said that I believe in the Holy Spirit to teach you in my absence, therefore, the Bible's purpose is clear to us here on earth. He gave Biblical Instructions Before Leaving Earth (Bible) to guide us in God's absence.

There were many nights, I would be laying down in the jungle with 1000s of thoughts, my mind racing out of my head and dreams from my childhood and I would see that cross with a crystal blue background in the sky.

Perhaps my purpose is to inspire others to come back into the good grace of God thus allowing them to experience the spiritual awareness within them. Many people never once consider helping others who are less fortunate; in my eyes, this is a sin. If you do not share your blessings from God, you show that you don't appreciate and respect His blessings.

God is not a God of convenience for you and no one else; some of us think you only call on God in your worst of times. What about calling on God to guide you when you're doing well in your life, 'at the top of your game,' not when you're down and out? We need to be thankful for all our blessings during our lifetime. I've learned how to appreciate my life and everything in this world, as well as having respect for others who have different beliefs or religions.

I discovered by showing compassion to others, your blessings from God will be plentiful. A spiritual awakening will give you the insight which will allow you to focus on keeping on the right path to complete the task God has chosen for you. Remember, God will not put any more on your plate then you can handle.

I was once told that I had a discerning spirit. I had no idea what that meant. I looked it up in a biblical dictionary. I was surprised to read that it is a spirit, which God gives to all of us. It is up to you how you use it. The power to ignite your spiritual awareness rests within you. Allow God to come into your life to create a clean heart and an open mind. Understand that positive actions will take you further in life than negative ones. While we are born in sin, only God's love and grace can set you free.

Always be mindful of how your actions contribute to your life and those around you and whether you are a part of the problem or a solution to the problem. Allow others to seek God and their spiritual awakenings as well, always help a person that wants to improve their life. A discerning spirit for others is a gift to heal or to see into the future.

My mother taught me as a small boy to believe in the Father in heaven versus man on earth. I have read the

Bible and the scriptures just about all my life. I realize some people use the Bible to brainwash people for-profit and to enrich themselves, and not for helping others in need. Such greed is a betrayal of God's sacrifice for man. Men have been doing this for centuries, interpreting the Bible for their benefit. The Bible can be interpreted in many ways, but I accept it as one teaching from God.

Be the best spokesperson you can be and always glorify God for giving you the blessings and love that have enriched your life. Only God can change a man's heart. Never disrespect God's blessings because it may never come back. Knowledge and understanding will allow you to grow in spirit and mind. Allow yourself to enhance what God has already given you at birth. Always strive to inspire others and to serve God to the best of your ability.

I tried to learn everything I could in the Bible about discipline because discipline can lead to knowledge and understanding.

Being a child born out of wedlock, I began to wonder why I was here on earth in the first place and what was to become of my life. I was determined to overcome the obstacles I faced and the burdens. I limited my potential many times.

During my childhood, most of my Sundays were spent in a Pentecostal church. At times I became bored and uninterested in going to church because I felt as though I was being forced to listen to the pastor sermons and to learn something from Sunday school. If we did not focus on the pastor's sermon with my mother sitting right next to us, she would give us that famous mother look. She would give you a nudge letting you know that she was getting displeased with us not paying attention. If you didn't get it together, then next came the elbow. If that didn't work, you could rest assured when you got home, mother would use her old burned up razor strap.

Despite the church's efforts to get rid of crime and the dysfunctional lifestyles that plague many families in low-income communities across America, church elders make sure the pastor and his wife are well-taken care of. However, a lot of elders do what they want to do.

There are a lot of Christians who read the Bible and don't understand the book. Maybe some Christians look at the pictures as I did when I was a young boy. There are many people with very little faith in God but go to church every Sunday, looking for a miracle through the scriptures. You can't read scriptures to get your blessings. You must pray and back it up with faith to receive your benefits.

I believe scriptures don't always relate to what's going on in the streets like telling you the winning lottery number. Black folks often play a number because they saw it in the Bible. I believe you can relate what is going on in your life to scriptures in the Bible. The Bible states that if you neglect to train and teach your child, you don't love your child or yourself (Proverbs 13:24). These are powerful words for parents. To love a child is to discipline a child because one of the benefits of discipline is to know right from wrong and helps him/her make good decisions as adults. It also helps to live a long and peaceful life (Hebrews12: 11, Proverbs 6:23, 10:17,12,15:5 15:32,19:18) The Good Book helps to build character in your child and drives out selfishness and mindsets such as 'the world revolves around me.' One of the most important things I've learned was to take the focus off the child, and teach the child to look outward to develop empathy and respect for all of God's creatures and humankind.

The absence of many fathers in households has had a tremendously adverse impact on families. Material things cannot be substituted for a father. A father has the responsibility to provide for his child(ren). It's about spending quality time bonding and molding what you have created so that when your child matures, he/she can make a positive contribution to society.

Women are having babies today out-of-wedlock, which contributes to this "Me-Me-Me" epidemic, and no one wants to accept responsibility or hold himself/herself accountable for raising bad and unruly children. We have got to do a better job in our communities of teaching young men to respect and value women. Each parent has a part to play in the growth of their child. If a parent ignores issues rather than addressing them directly, it does not teach children the consequences of their choices and actions.

We, as a community, must strive to do more to become a 'village' that nurtures children and shows them how to be respectful, responsible, disciplined, and promote healthy relationships between men, women, and children alongside all of God's creatures. This is my belief system.

CHAPTER 10
DEATH OF MY LOVE ONES

Grief can become overwhelming, and it's painful. But if you transform it into remembrance, you're honoring the person you lost and keeping a part of that person as a celebration of their life.

I've tried to understand how death affects people. What I discovered is people do accept the fact that they will pass away at some time. But the most important fact of living is the impression that you leave on people. It can have a profound effect on them; like my Uncle Conrad (Connie). The advice that Uncle Connie gave me about the GI bill was to buy a triplex, live in one unit, and rent the other two out; thus, I could live rent-free. He planted the seed of real estate investment in my mind at an early age.

Uncle Connie and his wife, Aunt Dorothy (Dot) lived in the McCullough Street projects. They had seven kids. Brenda, Patricia, Pamela, Michael, PJ, Stevie, and Ronald. They worked at the junior high school where Michael (my brother) and I attended. We had to walk on "eggshells" because they told my mother whenever my brother and I were in the principal's office. Back in the day, the family kept an eye on you and would tell on you. Bad news travels fast; walking in the door, my mother would already have the razor strap waiting for Michael and me.

Looking back today I am greatly thankful to Uncle Connie and Aunt Dot for the time they devoted to my brother and me. Thank you for your wisdom and love, I miss you, Uncle Connie. You may be physically absent, but your voice will remain in my mind and heart forever.

My brother, Marvin, went to mothers' house, and discovered her on the bathroom floor. He called 911 and they rushed her to Harbor Hospital in South Baltimore. She regained consciousness after a couple of days, but x-rays showed she had brain damage. After a couple of days, Mother seemed to be on the road to recovery. We all were encouraged when it appeared that she would regain her wits and good health and be on her feet in no time.

One day, I went to visit my mother as usual, and we had lunch together. We had an enjoyable visit. After eating, I left and went home, kissing my mother on the forehead. That evening my brother called me and told me that my mother passed away. I couldn't believe my ears. When I heard the words, I fell to my knees. A doctor told me there was bleeding on my mother's brain, which was the real cause of her death. It was a profound moment; I had a deep, deep sense of sadness. Not only did I lose my mother but my best friend. It felt like someone reached inside my chest and ripped my heart out. I felt so empty, so hollow, and so alone.

It was one of the most difficult days in my life when I learned my mother passed away. At that moment, my mind raced back to an earlier conversation I had with my mother. "Leroy, there is something in this house," she whispered in a low shaking voice. "What do you mean something in the house?" I asked. She said, "Yes, something is not right. Like something is not good," she continued in a low voice like not to have someone overhear our conversation. "Mother, there isn't anything in the house," I said as I walked around looking for something. At the time, I thought she was imagining things. Mother always felt there were stronger and negative forces that attacked people.

My Uncle RC, my mother's brother, made all the funeral arrangements. My mother was cremated with the flowers around her big picture.

I informed my biological father of my mother's passing. I was hoping that he would show up for the funeral or send some flowers to show his gratitude for her nurturing me, taking care of me, and being courageous enough to bring me in the world after what they both did. In my heart, I had hoped that Charles would show respect and perhaps show that he loved my mother at one time. One of the most disappointing times in my entire life was when Charles Walker, my father, did not show up for my mother's funeral. He didn't even send a card to the mother of his only son.

What kind of man would do this? Charles boldfaced lied to me, stating that he would send some flowers to the funeral. Charles, over the years, did many things to me, but this was the most significant act of betrayal to me. Charles Walker made another empty promise to me and disrespected my mother. Nothing had changed about Charles, and I knew now he would never change. I took serious offense to his broken promise, but given his track record, why should I have been upset?

This was just further proof that he never really wanted to be a father, never loved me, and his relationship with my mother was nothing but lust. He was never in love with my mother. When I approached my father, he came straight out and told me that he doesn't go to funerals. I have no respect for any man who can make a baby and not accept the responsibility that comes with it.

My father and I had significant differences, but I believe in moving on in life, you must forgive those who, in some way, have hurt you, my father was no exception. The older my father became, the more he started reaching out to me. The love of your parents sometimes is such a strange thing, and we don't get the opportunity to choose our parents.

I believe Charles' lifestyle and his need to control others and their money or what he thought was his money contributed to his demise. Charles went to great lengths to keep that control. Charles Walker was an 89-year-old man with a 40-year-old girlfriend who smoked crack and took Viagra to keep up with his young girlfriend. He bought crack to control her and let us not forget about Charles' wife, who had been a long-time heroin addict. Charles' wife was a principal of a high school and was attacked by some students who beat her up and threw her down the staircase. Her injuries were of such a severe nature they forced her to retire on medical leave, and she sued the school system with Charles' assistance. The Baltimore City school system settled, and Charles took control over her retirement money as well as her disability money. He became her caretaker, and everything would go directly to him to provide for her every need.

When my stepmother started to complain about constant pain and that the prescribed medication was no longer working, my father took drastic measures to keep control over my stepmother's money. She asked Charles to see her brother in East Baltimore to purchase illegal drugs to numb her pain. To the best of my knowledge, this continued for 15 years until Charles' death.

My sister Charlene would call me when she took Charles to the doctors when he started complaining about a little pain in his chest. My sister told me that one of his doctors, during a regular checkup, indicated that my father had several mini-strokes. The doctor told my father he had to slow his lifestyle down and start eating more bananas for the potassium. I began to stop by his house regularly to check up on him and see how he was doing. Charles was very weak and frail, not the same man that gave me lessons in life good and bad. I still had an emotional attachment to my father.

Charlene called me once again, stating Charles had to be admitted to the hospital. I raced over to the hospital as fast as I could, only to find Charles, setting up talking and getting fresh with one of the nurses. I asked him, "How are you feeling, Pops?" he looked at me "Great, I don't know what the big fuss is about." I stayed at the hospital for a while, talking to him and then left. Two hours later, I received another phone call from Charlene, "Leroy, the doctor called me. Dad has had a massive stroke." Leslie and I rushed to the hospital once again, only to see my father was emotionless. The only part of his body moving was his eyes. I tried everything in my power to communicate with my father. Charles just laid there, motionless. Charlene then calls our other half-sister, Kandi, the youngest daughter of Charles' three children. His prognosis was not good, Charlene called Charles' wife because the doctor who examined him, said it was time to transferred Charles to hospice. Everyone started to show up, even Charles' young girlfriend. Good heavens! Leslie and I thought things were going to explode with some drama, but after the shocking news from the doctor, it put us all in a state of grief. Leslie and I stood at the end of my father's bed. Leslie looked at me with a bit of surprised when he saw tears streaming down my face.

Yes, I found myself crying over this man. This man, who was incredibly selfish towards me, disrespectful and betrayed me, had tears rolling down my face for him the first time in my life. Looking at him, without being able to move a muscle, he started crying also. I guess at that time I forgave him, which was a profound moment for me.

I had a Jack Russell dog named Shorty. Shorty was my best friend, and we were just as content living with each other. However, to my surprise Shorty and my brother Leslie got along very well; you see Shorty wasn't the friendliest dog. Shorty and I missed his company when he moved to his new apartment.

About a year after Leslie left the house, Shorty got very sick, and the Veterinarian told me that Shorty had cancer. I looked at my little man (Shorty) in his eyes. I'm sure he did not know what was going on with him to make his body so weak. But during the last days of my dog's life, he would sleep in the bed with me and wake up in the morning with me. When I noticed that he stopped eating, I knew in my heart that the time was getting near. There are times we find ourselves in denial dealing with the inevitable like the situation with my dog.

When the day he could not stand, I picked him up and rush him over to the Veterinarian. Once I was there, one look from the Veterinarian told me that Shorty was dying. He told me to let him go gracefully. To see him suffering and in pain, without making a sound, I knew it was time to let him go. It was one of the hardest decisions I have made in my life, but the best. If dogs go to heaven, I know I will see Shorty again.

My brother Leslie was my other best friend, the one that knew me and accepted me as I was. He understood where I had been, accepted what I had become, and still gently allowed me to grow. He was also very close to my grandmother, as well as Marvin. After the passing of our grandmother Elsie, Leslie went into a deep tailspin. Everyone grieves differently; Leslie's grief became self-destructive. Leslie became homeless, and his addiction to drugs consumed him. He could never keep any money because all his money went to purchasing drugs.

I think my whole family started noticing his behavior, but no one cared about his wellbeing. When he was on his game, he was a good worker and held CDL licenses that allow him to drive large trucks and seemed too no problem getting a job. His challenge was keeping a job. He could not show up on time and could not pass a urine test. He struggled with this problem ever since coming back from serving in the military. I thought it was some form of depression or PTSD. Sometimes we would talk until the sun came up, we had so many memories. I probed and wanted to know the secret of why he could not control his drug addiction and seek help before it got too late. As always, he would laugh it off and say, "I got this under control."

Leslie was a no show at my mother's funeral. I was extremely angry with him for not paying respect to our mother. She deserved it after doing so much for him. When I finally caught up with Leslie, I question him as to what was so important that he couldn't make it to our mother's funeral. He confessed that he was so high that he couldn't make it to the funeral. His behavior was so out of order and he seemed to be lost to me, and I didn't understand.

Many years after my mother's death, knowing in my heart, my mother would have wanted me to reach out and do what I could to help my brother Leslie. After a couple of years of living on the street, he got a senior citizen apartment. We kept in contact with each other daily. However, when left alone, it seemed like his demons would take control.

He stopped paying his rent, and all the furniture that I gave him was sold for drugs. I was so hurt to see my brother in a situation like this; I invited him to stay in my home until he could get his life back together. He would have to obey my rule, living in my house drug-free. Requiring Leslie to live drug-free seemed to force the demons to stay away. He stayed with me for 18 months and was getting himself together. We were spending a lot of quality time together and bonding. He was there for me when my father had a massive stroke and died.

I thought Leslie had his feet firmly planted on the ground and was ready to move on. He displayed his independence, showed that he was able to put groceries in the refrigerator, keep a roof over his head and clothing on his back. Leslie decided to leave my house with my blessings. Once again, I helped him get some furniture so he could have a fresh start.

One day I was driving down Park Heights Avenue. I saw a guy on a walker that look like my brother. As I got closer, I knew it was my brother. I pulled to the side and ran to my brother and began to cry. I did not know that his health had deteriorated so much. I could see death in his face. I drove him home and asked him what he needed. He would ask for small things such as microwavable food, juices and breakfast food. I tried to insist that he go to the hospital to get treatment, but he adamantly refused several times. He used his social security and VA benefit checks he received the first of the month to buy drugs. On one occasion I did get him to agree for me to take him to the VA hospital emergency room. After the doctors examined him, they knew he was critical and tried everything to get him to stay for treatment. He refused and admitted that he was not afraid to dye. You cannot force a person that is of sound mind to accept treatment. During the days that follow, I would visit him and found him not to be able to move but he still refused to go to the hospital. Finally, I contacted social services and asked them to check on him; when they arrived, they found him on the floor and unable to get up on his own. They called 911 and he was still adamant about not going to the hospital. Social Services call the Police and they told him he did not have a choice he had to go to the hospital. He asked me not to leave him. I followed the ambulance to Sinai Hospital in Baltimore Maryland. I could see the fear and death in his face. His daughter, sister and close friends that cared about him arrived while he was in the emergency waiting to be admitted.

I received the call before he was admitted to the hospital that he had passed at 4:20 am. I was devasted, it seemed my heart dropped out of my chest. I felt like a failure because I could not help my brother to overcome his addiction. It took me years to understand that it was not my fault because it was his choice to use drugs. We all have choices.

Reflecting now, the death of my loved ones has had such a profound impact on my life. I have come to realize how fortunate I was to have a mother that was a strong-minded woman and a fighter. She did the best with what little she had and under complicated circumstances to raise my brothers, sister, and me. She will always be my hero. I owe a lot of gratitude to my mother. She made me the man who I am today because of her love and support.

After my mother passed away, I was going through her personal belongings and pictures, and I found a very old Bible that was on her nightstand. She kept all-important documents in this book. I noticed in that old beat-up Bible; mother had seven rules of wisdom on a page that was earmarked. It read like this:

'Seven Wisdom Keys.'

1. What you cannot tolerate, you cannot change.
2. What you respect you will attract.
3. What you make happen for others; God will make it happen for you.
4. The secret of your future is hidden in your daily routine.
5. You are rewarded in life by the kind of problems you are willing to solve for others.
6. If you insist on taking something God didn't give to you, it is not yours.
7. An uncommon seed will always create a unique harvest.

Reading these keys inspired me to want to make a difference in the lives of women that also suffer as she suffered most of her life.

CHAPTER 11
REACHING MY GOALS AND DREAMS

You can control your destiny with a simple personality test. Write on a piece of paper some of your characteristics for the next three days. The first day write down what you consider are your bad traits and put it in a private place. On the second day write down what you consider are your good traits and put it in the private place. On the third day write down what you would like to accomplish, with your life and place it in the private place. On the fourth day retrieve all three pieces of paper. Your real personality traits will be revealed to you. Ask yourself can you change anything you see that will give you a better life.

Stay away from the haters who try to diminish your ambition and steal your dreams. Remember small-minded people will go out of their way to sabotage your dreams when you turn your back. Let others lead small lives, but not you. Let others argue over little things, but not you. Let others cry over small hurts, but not you. Let others leave their future in someone else's hands, but not you. Continue to reach for the stars. The highest levels of achievement come from people who are centered, intuitive, creative, and self-reflective. People who know how to see a problem as an opportunity to create change also see one-person junk as another man's treasure.

Even as a small boy, I had an entrepreneurial spirit. My mother bought us a pair of clippers to cut hair so that we could make extra money by cutting other kids' hair in the neighborhood. Each one of us had our own clientele, but we shared the clippers. But I upped my game from my brothers and graduated from haircutting to carrying people's groceries.

I even sold flower seeds during the spring and was a caddie at the golf course in Baltimore County. In July, I would go blackberry picking along the train tracks. The trick was to squeeze the berries to get the juice and mix it with some water and honey. I would then freeze the blackberry mixture in the refrigerator for twenty-four hours and sell it as freezie pops. I grew up having a keen business sense out of the need to support my mother. This is one of my strongest attributes.

Will power is the key to being successful in life. Successful people strive to better their life no matter what the odds are against them. Being true to oneself, using will power and discipline are some of the keys to success that will help to overcome doubt and fear.

I jumped into the paper products industry and opened LA Distributors, partnering with Fort Howard Paper Manufacture as a supplier. For years I supplied restaurants and industrial companies with paper products. In the paper supply business, the competition was stiff and the overhead and maintenance of delivery trucks were just too much to bear, so I closed the company.

The recession hit, and the furniture store struggled, so I sold everything and closed my doors after five years. I felt a sense of defeat.

The golden rule to be successful in life is always put people before material things. Money is not GOD. This will help you develop a value system that understands the importance helping humanity.

A smart man learns from his mistakes and never makes that mistake again. But a wise man finds an intelligent man and learns from him how to avoid the mistake altogether.

Despite growing up around poverty and violence, I strived to make a difference in my family's financial situation. My story is a true story of having nothing and struggling just to put enough food on the table.

I learned early on that it is not about your SAT score but your determination and your ability to stay focus. Good orderly decisions are the center of balance in one's life.

Never use ill-gotten money to build your life or business: *Proverbs 13:11 says "Wealth gotten by vanity shall be diminished: but he that gathereth by labor shall increase".* You should strive to become debt-free: Proverbs 22:7 *"The rich rule over the poor, and the borrower is slave to the lender".* The right partner is more precious than rubies, *Proverbs 31:10-12 Who can find a virtuous woman for her price is far above rubies. The heart of her husband doth safely trust in her so that he shall have no need of spoil. She will do him good and not evil all the days of her life.*

Surviving in BMORE

CHAPTER 12
SELF-REFLECTION

I am the product of a dysfunctional household living in urban America. To those who can relate to my experience, please know that my heart goes out to you. I learned from my mistakes in life and decided to move forward with life. I knew where I came from, I used my ability to recognize my weakness, and made the necessary changes to succeed in life. Don't harbor ill feelings, don't be jealous of others success, respect yourself and others, or wallow in self-pity.

I believe that self-hate, jealousy, a lack of a value system, and lack of respect for others has been one massive 'plague' that has eroded the fabric of the American culture. Today's youth feel a sense of entitlement that only applies to them but not to others. They think everyone owes them something, and don't respect authority as I once did. They have even less respect for human life, and virtually all conflicts are resolved with guns and killing.

Respect is a two-way street. If you desire to be respected, you must give respect to earn the respect of others. Don't judge a person by their skin color, sexual orientation, economic status or their religion. You will never reach your goals with that mindset.

Growing up I never allowed myself to be influenced by baseball players, football players, basketballs, rappers or movie stars. I had to focus on my life and what was best for me based on my circumstances.

Reaching my goals in life was like charting a course on the ocean. I was my Captain and there were times when I had to navigate rough and deep waters. However, I did not allow my fear to dictate my destiny. My father once told me, a scared man will never accomplish anything, and a coward will never have anything. Once upon a time, steel men sailed wooden ships but today wooden men sail steel ships. Men are no longer defenders, protectors, supporters or warriors. We need to get back to being steel men.

When I visit museums, I always take a minute to reflect on the sacrifices and struggles people have made for the freedoms of men and women of all races and creed. The National Museum of African American History and Culture in Washington DC displays the struggle we have endured for freedom, respect, and dignity. I clearly understand that no one can change our history or come up with a simple remedy to fix the racism that plagues our country. It is up to us, the people, to rise above the hatred, the dysfunction, the crime, the drugs, and violence in the hood.

Using the Bible as a guide, we have a 'roadmap' to inner peace, but it's going to take a willingness to accept a change for the good. This would allow our children to see the world as a place of opportunity, instead of an place of resentment and anger. Never compromise on your values and do what is right.

My organization, NAVA, strives to bring awareness and understanding of people's behavior to prevent destructive behavior in our children.

Leroy Allen

.

ABOUT THE AUTHOR

I grew up in poverty and lived in urban America (The Hood). Not knowing where my next meal would come from inspired me to build a wagon and a shoeshine box to make money. Who knew the youngest of four would accept the responsibility of helping my mother provide for the family. Now, as a grown man, while looking back on my past +I am happy to be alive and thank God I survived.

I had many uncles who mentored me and helped to shape me into the man I became. Giving honor to my mother, Juanita Hayes Allen, I wanted to help women and children who are in abusive and dysfunctional relationships, so I started The National Fund For the Awareness of Violence Against Women and Children (Nava Fund). I wrote the book, *Surviving in Bmore*, to encourage others to reach beyond their circumstances and realize their full potential by focusing on where they are going, not where they came from. Nava Fund is a nonprofit public support organization, and all proceeds from the sale of my story will go to assisting Nava Fund with its efforts.

This is a true story of me overcoming obstacles and adversities in the hood and surviving in Baltimore. www.navafund.org.

Made in the USA
Middletown, DE
20 February 2022

61293907R00056